GHOSTS
OF THE
BLACKSTONE
VALLEY

GHOSTS
OF THE
BLACKSTONE VALLEY

THOMAS D'AGOSTINO & ARLENE NICHOLSON

Haunted America

Published by Haunted America
A Division of The History Press
Charleston, SC
www.historypress.com

Front cover photo by Seth Pincins.

First published 2018

Manufactured in the United States

ISBN 9781467139595

Library of Congress Control Number: 2018942449

This book is dedicated to our family and friends—thank you for all your love and support—and our fur people Gus, Buster, Freyabell, Trudy and Aura.

CONTENTS

ACKNOWLEDGEMENTS

This book would not be possible without the assistance of many people. Special thanks go out to Jim Ignasher; Rich and Ally Alarie; Seth Pincins; PTL Paranormal; the LaFleur family in Whitinsville; Deb Vickers of DLH Paranormal; Kathy Hartley and the Friends of the Hearthside in Lincoln, Rhode Island; Carl Johnson; Kelly Pincins; Lori and Marty of Slater Mill in Pawtucket; everyone at Waterfront Mary's; Keith and Sandra Johnson; Ken DeCosta; the Paranormal Bikers; Skip Gervais; the Greenville Public Library; Jeanne and Vance at Granville's Pub; Deb, Chris and everyone at the Tavern on Main in Chepachet; Kent Spottswood; Burrillville Historical Society; Emma Nadeau; the Jessie Smith Library in Burrillville; Brown and Hopkins Country Store; Stone Mill Antiques; Glocester Heritage Society; Blackstone Valley Historical Society; Cumberland Library; Tom Sanzi; the Uxbridge Free Library; Worcester Historical Museum; the Worcester Art Museum; and everyone else who was of invaluable assistance but chose to remain anonymous. Thanks everyone, and many happy haunts!

INTRODUCTION

Early settlers of the Blackstone Valley arrived in an untamed wilderness with hopes and dreams of building a new and better life for themselves and their families. They were aware of the countless obstacles that stood in their way, yet these hearty souls forged on and built their homes and villages, enduring the dangers and disease the New World relentlessly threw at them. Indian attacks, wild animals, hard living and poor farming conditions, coupled with the many deadly diseases that befell them made for a fragile existence. The spirits of those strong people who refused to give up in life seem to have remained long after their physical forms have turned to dust.

Through the centuries, New England has been a focal point for haunts. Many attribute the concentration of these ghostly sightings to a large number of underground streams and quartz that lie abundant in the region, creating a natural battery that helps perpetuate the ghostly phenomena. Then, of course, there are the legends, those stories that have a thread of truth running through them but became embellished over time to favor a more romantic New England flavor. The Blackstone Valley is no stranger to such legends. In fact, the region harbors some of the best that have ever been penned or narrated.

In later years, the Blackstone Valley would become the birthplace of the American Industrial Revolution. From the moment Samuel Slater started the water wheel of his factory on the Blackstone River to the present day, the region has been renowned for its mills and factories. Mill villages sprang up everywhere, and people flocked from all over to find work and build their American Dream. But it was not as glamorous as they had hoped. The hours were long and torturous. The conditions were dangerous and sometimes deadly, and many adults refused to leave their plows and stoop to such labor. Enter the children. While the adults worked their crops and preserved their larder, the children, as young as five, could become financially useful to the family by helping out in the local mills. A new era had come, and it would change the landscape of New England forever.

Such change was not without its tragedies and scarring of the premises where these people lived and worked. Many of the factories still hold the ghosts of those who either met a horrible fate or refuse to leave out of love for their achievement. But these are not the only ghosts of the valley. Wars, untimely deaths, disease and other hardships have left blemishes on the land that occasionally come back to haunt us.

Much of the valley has been preserved for the sake of history, but some of the little villages and sites have fallen to the ravages of time and progress. Many of the skeletons and remnants of old factories, homesteads, hospitals and taverns can still be seen jutting out of the woods or at the end of a grassy field. In many cases, those who once walked this earth in a mortal frame still tenant them. Farms, long gone and turned into neighborhoods, contain strange visages from the past that no one can explain until they research the history of the area and find the venerable skeletons in their closets.

The Blackstone Valley comprises twenty-five towns and cities in Massachusetts and Rhode Island. Each town has its own story to tell, and all are rich with history and character, but some boast a host of haunted places that have thrived throughout the history of the region. Some of these stories are well told perennial favorites while others are a bit more obscure. I strove to bring new accounts to the reader that were not chronicled in the previous tomes. In some cases, we have updated some of our previous accounts due to current investigations, new research or portions that were left untold due to page constraints. Tales of some of the more eclectic to the absolute mad will make you want to venture out yourself and discover the haunts that lurk within the confines of the valley and some just outside its borders. New England is certainly a strange place, and the Blackstone Valley is as rich as it gets with tales, legends and haunts.

Almost every place in this book is open for public visitation. Others can be seen from the road or at a distance that does not constitute trespassing. Please obey all rules and regulations of the particular places and be courteous. Someday you may want to return, as will others who wish to relish in the adventures that lie within this book.

BLACKSTONE

(SEE WOONSOCKET)

BURRILLVILLE

SHERMAN PLOT

New England is full of urban legends and stories that are told around the light of a campfire or dimly lit chamber. Many of these legends are spawned from actual events or people that made an impression upon the populace. Some are born of youthful pranks or a location that becomes ripe for a good ghost story. In the case of the Sherman Cemetery, all of the above seems to apply. Sherman Cemetery is located at a crossroad separated by a large tree. Raised up from the road by a stone barrier, the unmarked plot holds the remains of four members of the Sherman family and what looks like a small cellar hole. Although the birth dates of a few of the Sherman family are documented, no records of their deaths are recorded in the historical registers for the state. Some of the family members buried there can be traced to the mid- to late nineteenth century. Being on the border of Connecticut in the most northwest part of the state, the cemetery is listed in the state historical records as 001. Like most Rhode Island families, the Sherman clan buried their own and kept no record of exact plots. In most cases, fieldstones marked the final resting places for their loved ones, and this plot was no exception. The stones are either long sunken into the earth or may have been carted away at one point by legend trippers seeking a souvenir for their excursion into the dark borders of the Blackstone Valley.

It is known that Clark Sherman is buried there, but who else lies in repose with him is a matter of debate. One camp believes his three wives, Ellen, Caroline and Laura, make up the rest of the graves. Another side claims it is one wife, Laura, his daughter and the daughter's aunt. The state seems to believe the latter. Whatever the case, the spirit of Laura does not remain at rest. According to legend, if you circle her interment three times during the full moon and call out her name, her spirit will appear. She will hover over her grave silently and quiescent before vanishing into the darkness of the night. Those who witnessed this macabre event report Laura's ghost has even spoken faint words of discontent. Probably toward the condition of her final resting place. Many Burrillville residents have been startled or even frightened by who they believe is Laura standing at the edge of the plot gazing sullenly as they pass. When they look back, her ghost is no longer there.

If you decide to trek out to the small burying yard, you may have to make a few attempts to conjure Laura from the correct grave, for all that remains is the base of one gravestone and some indentations in the ground where the family is interred. The base of the lone gravestone has also been relocated toward the front of the plot. Good luck, and bring a witness, just in case.

THE INDIAN MAIDEN'S ETERNAL LOVE

This legend has been told for many years in the manner you are about to read. Although the historical facts may have been embellished through the years, the romantic telling of love, murder and subsequent haunting makes for a well-rounded campfire story.

In the Tarkiln section of Burrillville, there is frequently heard the ghostly voice of a woman echoing in the midnight air. The voice cries, "Where is my necklace?" Sometimes her apparition is spotted roaming among thickets just off Horse Head Trail. Who was she, and why does she eternally haunt this quiet little corner of the town?

Hannah Franke was a Nipmuc Indian hired to keep house for the Walmsley family, known to be Nipmuc as well. The Nipmuc Indians and the white settlers lived together in the little hamlet of Tarkiln—which was called Oak Valley at the time—in Burrillville, Rhode Island. John Smith brought his family to the beautiful land around 1700. The first industry was a tar kiln to make pitch and charcoal. The area steadily grew, and by 1815, Tarkiln boasted four mills, a tannery and a gristmill along with two hundred settlers in the village.

Written accounts indicate that Hannah Franke's father and mother died in a house fire when she was young. Her grandmother then took her in until she too passed, leaving poor Hannah alone in the world. A peddler from Vermont named John Burke frequented the area, selling his wares to the villagers. One day, he spotted the young woman and immediately fell head over heels in love. He made frequent trips to the village, each time with a special token of affection for the young and beautiful Hannah. At twenty-six years of age, he was a mild-mannered young gentleman when he gave Hannah, then seventeen years old, a special shell necklace. A lengthy courtship followed, and everyone knew the couple was destined for marriage. Burke had asked several times for her hand in marriage, but Hannah was reluctant to leave her home and move to Vermont. Yet the necklace remained around her neck as one of her prized possessions and a symbol of the deep love the couple shared.

In September 1831, John Burke came calling upon Hannah once more and again asked her to be his bride. This time, she accepted his proposal. Amasa E. and Thomas J. Walmsley were outraged by this mixed relationship and Burke's relentless courting of Hannah. Many times in the past, the Walmsley brothers had thrown Burke off their property in hopes of keeping him away from the young Indian maiden. Perhaps, as one record states, Thomas was hoping that Hannah would take a liking to him, but that was not to be. Either way, nineteen-year-old Hannah resigned as their housekeeper and packed her belongings for the journey to Vermont and the start of a new life. The two brothers pretended to be elated about the union and bade the couple sit and have a few drinks for celebration. They made much merriment, keeping the libations flowing until the young lovers had more than their share of liquor. John Burke and his soon-to-be bride left the Walmsley home on September 18, 1831, to begin their journey to Vermont. Unfortunately, it was a journey that never came to be.

The two lovers traversed down Horse Head Trail toward Log Road. When they reached the intersection, Amasa and Thomas were waiting for them in the woods. They attacked the couple, beating them mercilessly. Burke was able to break free and, in a desperate attempt to lure the two from Hannah, began running up the trail on the opposite side of Log Road. The brothers caught up with him and swiftly beheaded him with an axe. They then returned to where Hannah was struggling for her life and finished her off. Hannah, using all the strength she could conjure, dragged

Horsehead Trail, where the Walmsley brothers accosted Hannah Franke and John Burke. *Photo by Arlene Nicholson.*

herself to a large pine tree where she expired. In Indian lore, the spirits of the trees brought peace to those who were passing through the veil. A few locals traveling the trail discovered their bodies a few days later.

News traveled fast of the gruesome murders, creating a general fear within and around the village. A sister of the Walmsley brothers worked for J.D. Nichols, who lived just up the road from where the murders took place. She began to act nervous each time the incident was mentioned. Nichols became suspicious of her actions, feeling she might know more about the murders than she was letting on. He began to question her about the incident. She finally broke down and confessed that her brothers were responsible for the evil atrocity that befell the young couple. Others had already suspected Amasa of foul play, as they noticed him wandering around the village two days after the murders with blood on his shirt. When asked how the stains originated, he gave conflicting stories, none of which seemed convincing to those who queried him on the matter.

Amasa was arrested, tried and found guilty of the murders. He was hanged on June 1, 1832, at 10:45 a.m. Some records indicate that the execution took place in a hollow where Roger Williams Park now sits, while others state that it took place at Field's Point. The younger brother, Thomas, was also arrested for the murders, but it has been the popular belief he died when he fell from a wagon before justice could prevail.

Although justice may have been served, Hannah's spirit has not rested ever since that fateful day. She is still seen searching the woods endlessly

The graves of Hannah Franke and John Burke in the woods of Tarkiln. *Photo by Arlene Nicholson.*

for her lost love and her necklace. Residents have seen Hannah's ghost wandering the edge of the woods near Horse Head Trail and Log Road at all hours of the day and night.

If true love is eternal, then Hannah will not rest until she finds her soul mate and the gift that she so adored in life.

THE SWAMP BRIDE'S GHOST

Maureen Circle in Burrillville is a rural neighborhood populated with modern homes. The wooded area offers the perfect country setting, quiet and secluded. That is, until the screams and cries of an ethereal being break the tranquil atmosphere. The area is somewhat developed now, but it was not always that way. In the early 1800s, it was forests and farmland. Burrillville was a new town, having just annexed itself from Glocester in 1806.

Some of these accounts lost no impetus as they were passed down from one generation to the next while others seemed to fall by the wayside. Such is the lesser-known story of what the locals call the ghost of the swamp bride.

In the small village of Mapleville, part of the larger aforementioned town, there lived a man named Jonathan Cuttle. Cuttle owned a farm near the outskirts of the village. He soon met Katherine Donahue, and a courtship ensued. It was not long before the two were destined to make their eternal vows. Jonathan proposed to Katherine in August, and they began planning for a September wedding. Everything was perfect—or so they thought. There was one deep, sinister plot lying in the dark shadows of another person's mind. David Jones, a neighbor of the Donahues, had also fallen in love with Katherine. He made many proposals and advances toward her, but all were met with staunch refusal. Katherine had found her true love and would soon become Cuttle's wife. This rejection infuriated Jones, who took on the notion that if he could not have her, no one would.

One day, while Cuttle was pitching hay, Jones crept up to the side of the barn where, with a hunting knife in hand, he watched and waited for the moment he could strike his archrival. Cuttle put the pitchfork down for a moment and took a break. That is when Jones sprang from his hiding place and quickly grabbed the pitchfork, burying the tines into Cuttle's back.

Jones then went in search of the woman who had spurned him. Katherine had gone to the marsh with her brother. She was going to fetch water for the

Road where the Swamp Bride's ghost is seen. *Photo by Arlene Nicholson.*

home while her brother hunted for dinner. As she sat dreaming of her new life, a sharp, piercing pain ripped through her neck. It was the hunting knife of David Jones. She let out a blood-curdling scream before falling dead into the swamp. Her brother heard the scream and came running to her side, but it was too late. What became of Jones is now lost to antiquity, but since then, Katherine has haunted the place where she met her horrible fate. Residents of the neighborhood often report hearing hideous, unearthly screams emanating from the area where Katherine was killed. Those who live close to the scene of the tragedy have witnessed their rocking chairs begin to sway to and fro by themselves as if an invisible being is resting within the frames. A few older residents have witnessed or knew of someone who had witnessed the ghost of a woman in a long white dress covered with blood walking in the road near the swamp. The alarmed witness would quickly approach the woman in distress only to have her vanish upon confrontation.

THE GHOST OF ANNIE TRASK

"Divers Search for Missing Woman"

That is the title of a newspaper article that sparked the research and discovery of this next story. Heavy rains and flooding ravaged the area in May 2006.

In the center of Harrisville, a village of Burrillville, the Clear River raged, rapidly threatening to overflow its banks into the streets of the village. The major concern became apparent when at about 10:30 a.m., a man passing the area witnessed a woman descend the stairway toward the edge of the Clear River and disappear. The witness never saw the woman fall into the water, but he noticed she was no longer there. The man called the police, who responded with rescue crews. Lieutenant Kevin San Antonio later told reporters, "That person did not come back up the steps. All we know is that it is a female and she was seen by rescue personnel."

The rescue personnel included Harrisville Fire Department employees. They all claimed to have seen the woman in the water when they arrived, but then she mysteriously vanished. None of them ever got a good look at the woman. Divers were called to the scene while police boats searched downstream. Searchers waded waist-deep in the river while divers scoured the bottom. Others searched the banks, all in the driving rain. Police knocked on doors hoping to find clues to the woman's identity, but

The Clear River Bridge in Harrisville. *Photo by Arlene Nicholson.*

nothing conclusive turned up in either search. About 4:00 p.m., the search concluded, with no body having been found.

It soon became the consensus among the rescuers that what they witnessed may have been the sighting of some sort of ghostly phenomenon. It was suggested that this might have been a reenactment of a previous incident or what is normally termed as a *residual* or *atmospheric* haunting. It is an accepted theory among the scientific community that due to the magnetic properties of the earth, it is possible that a moment in time can be "recorded" and replay when atmospheric conditions are in alignment with the moment the incident was recorded.

During a visit to the historical society headquarters, an interesting story was discovered in the archives that shed light on the occurrence a few days before. The article was titled "The Sad Fate of Annie Trask" and dated May 6, 1904.

On May 6, 1904, two youths passing over the bridge that spans the Clear River near the Laurel Hill Yarn Company found a lady's pocketbook and umbrella on the side of the highway. Investigators determined they were the property of Annie Trask. The possessions were taken to the home of her brother-in-law, and a search began for the missing woman. It was discovered

Sad Fate of Annie Trask
May 6, 1904

Last Friday night shortly before 9 o'clock, two lads who were passing over the bridge near the mill of the Laurel Hill Yarn Co. found a ladies' pocketbook and umbrella beside the highway near the bridge. Investigation showed them to be the property of Miss Annie Trask, daughter of the late Abel and Mrs. Trask of Bridgeton. The articles were taken to the home of Miss Trask's brother-in-law, Durwood D. Bailey, and the whereabouts of Miss Trask were immediately sought. It was found she had left the home of William A. Inman where she was employed, early in the evening, presumably to visit Dr. Bruce who was her physician, and under whose care she had been for several weeks. A hasty inquiry made at Dr. Bruce's revealed the fact she had not visited his office that evening. Grave apprehensions for her safety were then felt by her people who feared that she had lost her life in the mill pond beside which her pocketbook and umbrella were found.

The assistance of friends and neighbors was at hand, and a search was instituted. A boat was secured, and the pond was dragged late into the night. Work was resumed soon after light and continued all day without result. While many felt that the search was fruitless, others were more sanguine, and Sunday morning the pond was drawn off. When there was but a small stream running over the bed of the pond, the body was discerned about forty feet from the bridge. The body was taken from its resting place and tenderly carried to Mr. Bailey's home, where it was later viewed by Medical Examiner Wilcox and permission given for its burial.

Several theories have been advanced as the cause of the sad fatality, yet whether it was accidental or done in a moment of temporary insanity can never be known. Miss Trask was a most

214

The sad fate of Annie Trask. *Courtesy of the Burrillville Historical Society.*

that she had left the home of her employer, William A. Inman, to pay a visit to a certain Dr. Bruce, as she had been under his care for some weeks.

Volunteers dragged the river and pond throughout the night and next day. When Trask's body was still not recovered, the pond was drawn off. When but a stream remained of the pond, her body was discovered about forty feet from the bridge. Although several theories were brought forth as to how Trask met her fate, none were ever proven, and her death has remained a mystery since.

It was 102 years almost to the day that the same torrential rains and flooding that took place in 1904 triggered the ghostly reenactment of the untimely demise of Annie Trask.

It appears Annie Trask may have been reliving the moment she met her unfortunate demise. Or was it just a residual, a remnant recorded in time to be played 102 years later? No woman was found in 2006—neither were there any reports of missing persons that may have fit the description of the woman seen descending into the water. It is believed that the passerby, the rescue personnel and everyone else who saw the event witnessed a rare appearance of the ghost of Annie Trask. There has not been another such storm in the region since. It can be concluded that the storm of 2006 was responsible for bringing the sad fate of Annie Trask into the present. Will another such storm replay that moment of 1904 as well?

HARRISVILLE LIBRARY

Adjacent to the Clear River Bridge sits the old Stillwater Mill complex. Construction began in 2007 to transform the mill and buildings into a cultural center billed as "the intellectual heart of Burrillville." A section of the complex became the Jessie M. Smith Memorial Library. The apartments are state-of-the-art and have a grand view of the Clear River. The interior of the complex is completely modern, while the outside retains original characteristics of a nineteenth-century mill. There are a few historical figures still making their presence known around the complex. People have witnessed the ghost of a child climbing the stairs in one of the buildings. A young boy is seen in the hallway of another section of the complex. The library is host to a few spirits. One, in particular, seems to have a disturbing effect on the staff, for all of them have either divorced or ended a relationship within a short time of becoming employed there.

One librarian blames it on Mary Smith, wife of Jessie Smith. Mrs. Smith drew and signed her will on February 6, 1894, then—on the fourteenth of the same month—hanged herself at her home in the village. In her will, she left money and annuities to her housekeepers and siblings as well as funds for monuments and graves. After she mentioned all of the recipients of her fortune, the balance went to the Town of Burrillville for a library. The account was named the Jessie Smith Fund, and when it accumulated enough money, a proper library was to be built and a large portrait of Mrs. Smith and her beloved husband was to be displayed along with other photographs and personal possessions as a small memorial to the couple. According to some of the staff, Mrs. Smith was devastated by the loss of her husband and became melancholy over it. Her spirit now looks over her dowry and the staff. People have heard a woman's voice clearly emanating from vacant areas of the rooms. Books are often moved from one place to another without the aid of human hands. Sometimes books will fall off the shelves as if someone was intentionally dropping them. As far as the reason for the staff's relationship changes, they conclude that Mrs. Smith is just watching over their love interests.

If you visit the library, you may receive a piece of advice from the spirit of Mrs. Smith.

THE LITTLE SERVANT GIRL

Mark Teeter, a local musician, related this next account. Several years ago, he had an arrangement as a winter house sitter for a family that spent summers on their farm in Burrillville and winters in the warm South. The owner bought the estate to savor the beautiful New England spring and summer but deplored the harsh winters of the region. For eight years, Mark, who had no problem toughing out the winters, stayed at the house, tidying up, taking care of the farm critters and keeping the place in good repair. It was during one of those tenures that Mark arrived at the home and noticed the dining room had been decorated with the most interesting artifacts.

The owner of the home, while digging a foundation, uncovered an assortment of chains, shackles and other irons that would have been used many years ago to hold prisoners. Not knowing their actual use or how they were tied to the property, he hung them on the wall for display. The owner felt compelled to display them because they were part of the estate and therefore a piece of the farm's history.

The usual quiet winter days in the house Mark had grown used to over the years were interrupted by some unknown entity now residing within its walls. He would hear footsteps around the home and what seemed like voices echoing through the rooms. Old houses are prone to creak and moan, especially when the temperature changes.

One night, shortly after moving in, Mark was sitting at the kitchen table when the air suddenly became cold and chilled him immediately to the bone. He quickly turned toward the door, where something had caught his eye. It appeared to be a young girl about twelve or thirteen years old in a long, dirty dress and no shoes standing in the doorway.

The sight of the girl immediately took him by surprise, as she had suddenly appeared before him. She stared at him for about ten seconds and continued down the hallway. Mark related that he turned blue and bolted out of the house. He called his friend Ryan, who helped him on occasion with the house sitting. Ryan arrived and, upon investigating, found the house empty of any such person.

Ryan divulged that he had seen the little girl before and had heard footsteps shuffle by him on occasion. That was one reason why he would no longer enter the house alone. The two surmised that the old equipment on the walls was the reason the ghosts were suddenly making themselves known. They took the artifacts down and put them in a closet. For the rest of the winter, the phantom footsteps and ghost of the little girl bothered them no more.

THE PERRON HOUSE

By now, most everyone is aware of the famous Perron house and the events that transpired in the years they resided in the haunted domicile. The story of the family is now world-famous thanks to a book series and hit movie, *The Conjuring*, but lesser known are the events that took place before they owned the home.

The farmhouse was built in 1736, and eight generations of the Arnold family occupied the home. Even before the Perrons lived there, it was reported to harbor evil spirits. Tragedy plagued the Arnold family in the many years they lived there. Mrs. John Arnold hanged herself in the barn at the ripe old age of ninety-three years old. There were other suicides by hanging and poisoning as well as the murder of eleven-year-old Prudence Arnold, whose killer was never brought to justice. A beggar was given refuge from the bitter cold in one of the sheds on the property. The next morning, his frozen body was found bundled under a bail of hay. Another man met the same fate when, for some reason, he fell asleep in front of the house on his wagon. Two other men also mysteriously froze to death on the property, and two more drowned in the nearby Round Top Brook behind the house.

A former alleged Satanist and witch named Bathsheba Sherman hanged herself from a tree behind the barn in the late nineteenth century. According to the Perrons, she was the evilest of the entities that resided in the home. She was once accused of killing her baby as a sacrifice to the "dark one" but was acquitted for lack of evidence. She was believed to have had three more children, but all died before their fifth birthday. Born in 1812, Bathsheba took her own life on May 25, 1885.

Other former owners have seen an old woman in a gray dress with her head hanging to one side shrieking, "GET OUT, GET OUT, OR I WILL DRIVE YOU OUT WITH DEATH AND GLOOM!!!"

Another party purchased the home in 1983 and witnessed minimal experiences that tapered off over time. If you would like to read more about the home, pick up *House of Darkness: House of Light*, by Andrea Perron. Her chronicles of the family's ten years in the home are worth a read.

Note: The home is on private property and is off limits to any unsolicited visitors.

CUMBERLAND

ELDER BALLOU MEETINGHOUSE CEMETERY

Elder Ballou Cemetery is considered the most haunted final resting place in the Blackstone Valley. It is certainly worthy of being very close if not number one.

Cumberland Historical Cemetery #26 holds seventy-seven identifiable burials with sixty-six inscriptions, but there are over four hundred burials listed in the master index. Obidiah Ballou originally set aside the land specifically for the burying yard. Obidiah later gifted the land that he owned to his son Abner, excluding the burial ground. Obidiah's gift, with the exclusion of "one-half acre…which is, and I do hereby except it for a burying place for myself and my friends and neighbors," was recorded on March 23, 1749. On March 22, 1749, James Ballou donated the "Hallowed little site" across from the burying ground on which the meetinghouse was to be built.

The meetinghouse stood across the road from the burial yard until the 1960s, when it burned down. There is a marker on the spot where the building once stood. As for the cemetery, many will not dare traverse those grounds in the light of day or the hours of darkness. At the entrance of the burying yard sits a series of storage crypts (or keeps as they were once called) that were once used during the winter to store the deceased until the spring thaw enabled proper burial. The sight of these alone can cause visitors to

Elder Ballou Cemetery looks ominous even in the daylight. *Photo by Arlene Nicholson.*

shudder and abandon their original intention of exploring the morbid place of repose. The stones are strewn almost haphazardly about the hill, leaning perilously to and fro among the high grass surrounding them.

Then there is the ghost of the burial ground: the apparition of a man in gray often seen wandering among the tombstones. The misty form meanders about the edge of the knoll before disappearing over the crest.

A small group decided to embark on a legend trip about Cumberland and witnessed this unidentified apparition firsthand on a snowy night. The parking area across the road from the cemetery provided ample view of the graveyard without venturing into the cold. The snow had ceased, and a light wind blew—yet all was still within the burying yard. Suddenly, a figure came into view near some stones at the top of the hill. The figure, dressed in a dreary-looking uniform, seemed to be looking for something. It was concluded he might have been the owner of the farm located behind the cemetery. Some of the group exited the automobile in hopes of finding out more about the legend of the "man in gray." The snow was knee-deep, and traversing the hill was difficult. As one member of the group neared the top of the hill, the apparition vanished from sight. Not only was the strangely dressed figure nowhere to be seen, but the freshly fallen, knee-deep snow where he had just walked also was untouched.

The Elder Ballou Meetinghouse. *From Thomas D'Agostino's private collection.*

The Blackstone Valley Tourism Council hosted a Myths and Mysteries Tour in 2012, and one of the stops was Elder Ballou. During the visit, a recording session was arranged to see if anyone wanted to speak with the tour group. The grave of Cyrus Ballou on the hill above the crypts is said to be a hot spot for paranormal activity. It sits directly above the keeps. Lieutenant Ballou (circa 1790–March 7,1816) served some time in the military, and a small flag marks his gravesite. Someone in the assembly, facing away from the grave, asked, "Where are you now?" When the recorder was played back, there was a voice that answered, "Right behind you!"

Nine Men's Misery

Recently, there has been a renewed interest in one of my perennial favorites. In the woods of Cumberland, Rhode Island, sits a small pile of cemented stones fronted by a plaque. The tomblike structure is a memorial to nine men who were captured and slain by Native Americans during what has become known as Pierce's Fight, which took place during what we now call King Philip's War.

King Philip's War officially began on June 24, 1675, when the local Pokanoket Indians raided the village of Swansea in a retaliatory move against the colonists' aggression toward their people. The Indians killed seven colonists, decapitated them and placed the severed heads on sticks at the shore of the Kickimuit River. From there, the violence escalated to a full declaration of war. Philip (Metacom) and his followers wreaked havoc on the English settlements—but not without a heavy price. According to many historians, King Philip's War was the bloodiest battle ever fought on New England soil. Both sides burned villages and mercilessly slew women and children in the melee.

During the height of the conflict, a brutal battle took place along the banks of the Blackstone River. This battle came to be known as Pierce's Fight. On the morning of March 26, 1676, Captain Michael Pierce and his Rehoboth Militia were chasing down Cononchet and his marauders. When they arrived at the banks of the Blackstone River, they noticed what looked like some of Cononchet's warriors wounded and limping along a trail in the woods. The group of sixty-two English and converted Indians chased down the injured warriors, only to find they were decoys. The enemy came out of everywhere, completely surrounding the small band of Pierce's men.

Pierce quickly ordered his men to form a circle several deep, but it was to no avail, as the Indians charged at them eight-men deep. Pierce fell early in the fight, and for hours, the men gallantly fought without their leader, knowing they were doomed. When a few men remained, they broke rank and fled. Nine men were captured by the Indians and marched three miles to the spot now known as Nine Men's Misery. No one knows exactly what transpired, but it is accepted that the Indians sat the prisoners on a large boulder, and they built a fire. From there, the victorious Indians performed a dance and dispatched the prisoners with their tomahawks. Contrary to some claims, they were not beheaded and their heads placed on poles. The Bucklin Society recorded:

> *When the nine were found they were buried on the same spot they perished, somewhere near the monument. In 1790, A Dr. Bowen of Providence began to disinter the remains in search for one man, Benjamin Bucklin. It was known that this Rehoboth Militiaman was of extraordinary size and had a double set of teeth. One of the skeletons dug up was of extraordinary size, and by the fact of it's having a double set of teeth, was recognized as that of Benjamin Bucklin (Buckland), of Rehoboth. It is assured thus that the men were from other colonies than that of Providence.*

The locals found out and interrupted the disinterment, but not before the doctor had found what he was looking for. John Low is another claimed to be buried there. The others who were killed remain a mystery. It can be sure there were no French names, as the English and French were mortal enemies.

Benjamin Bucklin was thirty-five years old when he died and had married Rachel Wheatley Allen in November 1663. They had several children, but none were known to be of his stature. In 1928, the remains of the nine men were dug up and transported in a crate to be stored by the Rhode Island Historical Society. It appeared that the Trappist monks, owners of the land at the time, objected to having an unconsecrated burial on their property. The crate stayed unopened with the society until 1976, when the remains were reinterred at the present location. This was the 300th anniversary of the fight and the 200th anniversary of our independence.

Such events have left a permanent scar on the area, as the place is haunted by not one but several spirits. Screams have been heard echoing through the woods around the monument. The screams resemble those of someone in mortal agony. The ghost of a small child is seen near the swamp just to the left of the monument. There are remains of a home and signs that the area was once a farm. She could be a ghost of one of the many casualties of the war. There are claims that a child drowned in the swamp many years ago, but records have not surfaced to verify that as of yet. A ghostly rider has been known to suddenly appear on the trail and wisp off into the void. The sound of galloping and a horse whinnying presages the appearance of the phantom rider. The trails are easily discerned for some distance and the woods sparse enough where a horse and rider could not find camouflage from curious eyes without great difficulty. One person was at the monument when she heard muffled screams that sounded more like the deadly battle was being replayed centuries after it had originally taken place. Mary Dougherty was visiting the site in 1976 when she was suddenly taken aback by the ethereal cries the area is now famous for.

If you decide to hike out to the monument, start at the trail just over the guardrail and stay to the right, then follow the red markers. While you are there, you may want to check out the library, as it also is haunted. The building was once home to a Cistercian monastery. In 1900, John Mary Murphy purchased 530 acres of land, and he and his brothers began building one of the first Trappist monasteries in the United States. The church was finished in 1928, but a fire in 1950 put an end to the monks' tenure in Cumberland. The group moved to Spencer, Massachusetts, where they still reside, growing their own food and making preserves, beer and everything else they need to survive by their own hands. Visitors can purchase some of their creations at the gift shop on the premises.

As for the former monastery, it now houses the Cumberland Library. Although the monks are long gone, some of their ethereal brethren still linger within the walls of their old home. One particular ghost likes to close books left open on the tables in the library. People hear voices and doors slamming, and have seen shadows move about the large staircase leading to the other floors. One staff member heard a voice call her full name. This was somewhat unsettling, as no one she worked with ever acknowledged her in that manner.

A former Trappist monk reported that while he was living at the monastery, he often heard, in the dark hours, the sound of what appeared to be hammering on rocks. His superiors told him the sound was the spirits of the former inhabitants still working on the building. Another former monk corroborated a correspondence we received from a man who now lives in the Midwest. The Midwesterner also was a former member of the society and was eager to share an interesting story. In his letter, he stated the group moved to Spencer and, once settled, started the process to reclaim their deceased from the Cumberland grounds. When a brother died, he would

Nine Men's Misery Monument in the woods of the monastery in Cumberland. *Photo by Arlene Nicholson.*

The old monastery is still haunted by some of the monks who lived and died there. *Courtesy of Seth Pincins.*

be laid upon a simple board and covered only with a shroud before being interred in the earth. In that way, all could go back to dust in a natural way.

A construction company was called in to carefully excavate the burial site for removal to the new monastery. When they exhumed the first burial, work stopped. Everyone present was awed by the fact that the body was in a perfectly preserved state. It appeared he had not gone back to the earth at all. During our tour, a man came forward and stated that it was his father who was hired to dig up the bodies and move them. The workers unearthed the first grave and found that the body was almost untouched by death after more than half a century. The driver of the backhoe, being religious and perhaps a bit superstitious, exited the machine, refusing to continue. Several of the workers dropped their tools and sided with the backhoe driver, refusing to finish the job.

Despite the ghosts, the grounds of the monastery are beautiful, with a serene, welcoming atmosphere. One should take time to savor the history that lingers and, of course, the spirits.

TOWER HILL ROAD

Cumberland, Rhode Island's Ghostly Throughway

Ghosts and apparitions have become a part of our daily lives. Not a day goes by where there isn't someone who has a story to tell of their experience with those from the other side of the veil. If you find yourself traveling through Cumberland, Rhode Island, take a moment to roll down Tower Hill Road. It seems there are a lot of ghosts that have made this small, winding road their eternal address.

The ghost of a little girl is most frequently spied sitting in the front yard of an old farmhouse. Motorists often slow down to get a better look at the strange apparition dressed in older period clothing. The girl then either vanishes or just sits there unaware of the spectators' presence.

On the sharpest curve of the road is the spirit of a little boy running with his dog. He was hit and killed on the treacherous curve many years ago. Accidents of that nature are common on this dangerous track of the road. The curve will sneak up on the unwary motorist, so beware. The origin and identity regarding several of the ghosts on Tower Hill Road remain shrouded in mystery, but there are records of actual incidents that would explain some of the haunts of the road.

A phantom toddler on a tricycle has been spotted in the woods surrounding the snaking lane. The child was struck and killed by a car while he was riding his tricycle. A guardrail was put in place after the incident to prevent other such tragedies. Many people tell of feeling a presence with them while traveling down this road. Various people swear they will never drive down the road again, while others continue to seek a glimpse of the ghosts that roam the country lane.

CUMBERLAND'S STRANGE REQUEST

Town council meetings can sometimes have some pretty strange requests. Sometimes it is a noise ordinance to stop peacocks from screeching. It may be a citizen who does not like certain signs posted or parking in a particular area on a street. One of the strangest requests comes early in our nation's history. The following request was recorded at the very first town council meeting held in Cumberland, Rhode Island, on February 8, 1796:

Mr. Stephen Staples of Cumberland appeared before this council and prayed that he might have liberty granted unto him to dig up the body of his dofter [daughter] *Abigail Staples late of Cumberland single woman deceased in order to try an experiment on Livina Chace wife of Stephen Chace which said Livina was sister to said Abigail deceased which being duly considered it is voted And resolved that the said Stephen Staples have liberty to dig up the body of the said Abigail deceased and after trying the experiment as aforesaid that he bury the body of the said Abigail in a deasent* [decent] *manner.*

That is what was entered into town records. We know that Abigail Staples was born January 26, 1773, and died about 1795, most likely of consumption. Consumption was what we now call tuberculosis. Whole families were wiped out by the malady, which held New England in the grip of fear for over a century. The people feared those who died from the disease were returning not in body but in spirit and feeding on the surviving members of the family, and as long as the body remained whole or decomposing in the grave, the spirit would feed upon the living and return to the grave to nourish the rotting corpse.

They were called spectral ghouls, and the only way to stop the ghouls from their nightly carnage was to exhume the body, cut out the vitals and burn them. In many cases, the ashes of the burned remains were fed to the sick with medicine. This hysteria lasted until 1892 as far as we know, terminating with the case of Mercy Brown in Exeter, Rhode Island.

The Staples Lot where Abigail Staples is buried in an unmarked grave. *Photo by Arlene Nicholson.*

Incidentally, there is no record of what Staples did or the outcome of the experiment. The Staples lot on Nate Whipple Highway in Cumberland has many plain fieldstone markers, so the exact whereabouts of Abigail's grave is lost to antiquity.

So, next time you attend a town council meeting, think about the strange requests from citizens, then think back to the request once asked in Cumberland. I am sure they will not compare.

GLOCESTER

THE STONE MILL IN CHEPACHET, RHODE ISLAND

It is no secret that the Blackstone Valley region is home to many old mills. Some are but memories; others are still in use for manufacturing, and others cleverly redesigned to serve another purpose more akin to modern society. One such structure is now known as Old Stone Mill Antiques on Putnam Pike in Chepachet, Rhode Island.

Lawton Owen built the mill in 1814 for the Chepachet Manufacturing Company. The structure stood three stories high from the street level with a gabled roof and belfry. Owen's mill produced cotton cloth until Sayles and Smith gained control in 1864. The new owners introduced wool to the process to create cassimere and satinet.

After the Great Freshet of 1867, the third floor and gabled roof were removed, and a flat roof was laid down, making the structure smaller and stronger. The business grew, as did the size of the mill. At one point, the building was four times the size of what is seen today.

The original stone section was the picker mill, a dangerous and unhealthy place to work. The workers constantly inhaled the dust and flying debris that permeated the air from the machines cleaning the wool. It can be assured many workers became ill from the hazardous working conditions. Children employed in the mill often met with tragic fate while working the unforgiving machines or repairing broken threads on the looms. All in all, early mills were not very worker friendly.

Stone Mill Antiques on the Putnam Pike in Chepachet. *Photo by Arlene Nicholson.*

In 1925, the owner tried to burn the mill for insurance, but diligent neighbors quickly quelled the blaze before too much damage was sustained. The mill continued operations as the Glocester Yarn Company before finally closing its doors in 1969 after 155 years of manufacturing. In 1982, the wooden additions were demolished for safety reasons, leaving the original stone section of the mill awaiting a new life. The new life would be in antiques.

Although several owners subsequently owned the mill, Deb LaCarron was the one who felt an uncanny connection with the building from the first time she drove by the then-vacant building. "I remember driving by this place many times saying to myself, 'I am going to own that building one day.'"

It was many years later when the building went up for sale that she would be able to fulfill her dream and purchase the old mill. From there, she and her husband, Larry, began to renovate and set up shop. It was not long before they found out they were not the only ones who tenanted the place. One particular night, Deb left early, being very tired. Larry stayed and continued working in the quiet of the night. While Larry was downstairs working, he was startled by the pitter-patter of footsteps running around on the second floor. As he walked toward the center of the main floor, he distinctly heard the footsteps again, accompanied by the giggling of a little child. He knew he was alone, or at least no other living person was in the building with him. He went upstairs to investigate the source of the noises but saw no one else in the open rooms. It was then he decided to call it a night and left.

The main door has a padlock and a heavy lift-style latch to keep the door closed once unlocked. One night, the ghosts decided to play games with the door, sealing Larry in and Deb out. Larry could not open the door, despite ramming it with full force while Deb pulled on the handle from the outside. Finally, the door swung open by itself, leaving the couple both stunned and bewildered.

On one occasion, Deb went upstairs to arrange some of the antiques. As she started turning off the lights, she came face-to-face with the glowing form of a little boy. The misty figure reached out its hand in her direction. Deb became startled, but she was not so much frightened as curious as to what the child wanted. She stood there and stared in half disbelief at the glowing apparition. It finally faded away in front of her. Deb stated that on many occasions, she gets the feeling that there is someone else in the building with her. Many customers have come down the stairs perplexed over the fact that they heard footsteps behind them and had turned around only to find they are the only ones there.

Upstairs room where Deb saw the ghost of a little child. *Photo by Arlene Nicholson.*

People shopping for antiques in the building have confided in Deb that they could feel something in certain areas. The spirits are not a threat but rather happy the mill is being used for such a purpose. "It seems they just want to let us know that they are here and are not trying to scare us but are happy we are here with them," Deb said.

John Joseph Thibodeau works at the mill, keeping things in order. Many times, he is alone in the old building fixing something or just tidying up the exhibits. Quite often, he has heard what appears to be sounds of children running around in the mill:

> *When I am here alone, and it is quiet, I often hear a noise or voice and I will turn the radio off. You can actually hear footsteps going up the stairs and voices of children on the second floor. Other people have come in and heard them while shopping. As you know, children worked in these mills many years ago before the child labor laws.*

No one has been able to find the identity of the ghosts that reside in the mill and like to make their presence known. Perhaps they are happy that it is an antique shop where they may be more at home with the fashions and trends of their time.

During the Christmas season, the village hosts candlelight shopping on the three Thursdays before Christmas. We always pick one of those Thursdays to visit the store and chat with everyone. Depending on the time, you can hear the laughter and footsteps of the living passing through looking for that perfect gift, but later, when the crowds dwindle and the candles burn down…

ARNOLD STAPLES

Two Cemeteries and Three Graves

Although not exactly a ghost story, this next account is fascinating. New England is full of tales where people had their graves dug and their stone in place before they died just to make sure it was going to be the way they wanted. Arnold Staples of Smithfield was one of those folks.

Staples, a retired undertaker, knew what he wanted for his eternal repose. In 1911, the eighty-nine-year-old man dug his own grave to make

Staples stone in Acotes Cemetery. *Photo by Arlene Nicholson.*

sure it was to his liking. His wife died on December 10, 1877, and Staples, being a sentimental sort, decided to brave the elements and dig the frozen ground on that particular day. Not long after he completed his task, heavy rains caved the hole in, forcing poor Arnold to once again dig his final resting place. This time, he fortified the hole with supports to keep the grave from collapsing.

Staples died on July 1, 1913, and was buried next to his wife in the grave he had twice dug for himself. This interment did not last as long as he would have expected, for in 1934, family members had his remains, along with those of his wife and children, removed to Acotes Cemetery in Chepachet. He is mentioned in the Rhode Island Cemetery records as being interred in Smithfield Cemetery SM084 and Glocester Cemetery GL023. So not only is Mr. Staples recorded as buried in two different places, he also had three graves dug in order for him to rest in peace.

Brown and Hopkins Eternal Patrons

Chepachet, Rhode Island, is known for its preserved beauty and rustic charm. Historic taverns, homes and businesses lace both sides of Route 44, beckoning the curious to inspect what time and progress have failed to spoil. Along with these old structures are many remnants of the past, including ghosts still lingering among the antiquated walls of these edifices.

One such place is Brown and Hopkins General Store. In 1799, Timothy Wilmarth built the structure as a private home. Ira Evans purchased the home in 1809 and turned it into a general store. James Brown and William Hopkins owned the store from 1921 to 1964, when the Steere family took the reins. Several owners have made their mark in one of America's oldest continuously running stores. In 2004, Elizabeth Yuill purchased the store, keeping the tradition alive. B&H boasts old-fashioned delights, handmade items and many other products that bring the customer back to times when life was simple and slower.

With the building also came a few resident ghosts. The ghosts have a penchant for rearranging things. Employees enter the store in the morning and often find certain items in complete disarray, such as scarves or hats that appeared to have been tried on and discarded during the witching hours of the night. Voices are often heard around the rooms that are uninhabited by humans, and footsteps on the second and third floors

Brown and Hopkins General Store on the Putnam Pike in Chepachet. *Photo by Arlene Nicholson.*

resound when they are otherwise empty. A few of the staff have heard people upstairs mulling around after closing time, but upon ascending the only staircase to let their customers know it was past store hours, not a living soul would be found anywhere.

A few women shopping on the second floor descended the stairs while two other customers were heading upstairs. One of them said: "If you are going up there, I'd be careful. We just heard someone talking and walking around in the old bedroom, but there was no one in the room when we entered. I am not surprised this place is haunted."

Liz had several stories to tell, but the one that struck her as most memorable was when she and a staff member were redecorating the bedroom on the second floor. There was a chandelier in the corner that had been there a while:

> *Trish and I were up in the bedroom. We were moving a chandelier from one corner of the bedroom to the other figuring it hasn't sold; let's give it a new home. I took it down and was carrying it from the chain links. I was walking, and I could feel somebody tugging on it. I stopped, and I was pulling on it, and I am looking at it and it is not hanging down, it*

Bedroom where the ghost of a little girl is seen. *Photo by Arlene Nicholson.*

> *is literally angled like someone was trying to pull it out of my hand. So I rested it down on a small table and almost immediately it started spinning in circles as if someone was playing with it.*

Staff member Bonnie Godin had a few stories to tell. She had never had a paranormal experience until she started working at the store:

> *I was working over here (in the back room on the first floor), and I felt a very cold breeze. I thought it was the air conditioner, so I moved, but when I moved, the air followed me, and the hair on my neck went up. I was talking to a lady, and she asked, "Who else is here?" And she makes a gesture of a ghost. So I tell her about the bedroom and the fireplace where they are most active. The lady then says, "There is something that is following you right here, right now." She then stated that whatever it was that was in here with me was not comfortable with her, and it wanted to be near me.*

Bonnie also remembered a man and woman who mentioned the presence of a little girl with long blonde hair and blue eyes who died of a respiratory illness in the bedroom. That might explain why the chandelier was being pulled from below at the height of a child and not lifted to adult height when Liz was carrying it. The little girl is called Abigail by the staff. But there is another ghost residing upstairs, a woman they call by the name of Ella.

Bonnie had been working at the store just a few weeks when she had her first experience. She was upstairs in the dining room by herself when she suddenly heard crying coming from behind her. She looked around, but there was no one else up on the second floor. She went downstairs a bit shaken and told Trish what had just happened. Trish looked at her with a straight face and said, "Oh, that's just Ella." Bonnie replied, "You do not understand, there is nobody up there." Which was followed by Trish telling her, "It's Ella the ghost, Bonnie."

Roberta Merlino attested to having someone tug her coat while shopping on the second floor. She mentioned the incident to her husband, Ed, who in turn relayed the incident to the staff. Liz and company reassured them the ghost was real but completely harmless.

One Christmas, Bonnie was on the third floor where the decorations are kept, retrieving some for the season, when she saw a dark form move from one end of the room to the next.

Several years ago, Liz asked Arlene and me, along with our friends Rich and Ally Alarie, to document the ghosts and spirits of the store. One of the resident ghosts likes to hide on the third floor, which was unoccupied at the time. Cameras and recorders were set up overnight to record any activity without our disruption. Subsequent evidence captured proved that the building has some permanent guests.

Although the cameras failed to pick up any visible evidence, recorders captured voices of children, a mother calling her daughter, footsteps creaking on the stairs and other unexplainable sharp, loud noises within the building. The ghosts seemed to prefer being heard and not seen on that occasion. According to everyone at Brown and Hopkins, they are not harmful in any way, just a part of the charm that makes the store a place to visit over and over again.

Brown and Hopkins store is on Route 44 in the center of Chepachet, just over the bridge from Stone Mill Antiques.

DORR DRIVE

Gloucester Light Infantry Armory

The armory on Dorr Drive behind the town hall was once part of a schoolhouse. A section of the building burned down long ago, and the remaining portion of the historic building now houses the Gloucester Light Infantry reenactment equipment. It also houses one of its former students who met with tragedy many years ago.

While the building was being used as a schoolhouse, students were obliged to attend their daily lessons. One day, a student left the building in a hurry, bolting across Dorr Drive into Douglas Hook Road without looking to see if any horses or wagons were coming down the road. Unfortunately, a carriage traveling toward the main pike struck the youth, running him over and killing him.

Witnesses, including some of the infantry reenactors, have seen the visage of the boy emerging from the building and running out into the street before vanishing into thin air. Tom Sanzi of the Gloucester Light Infantry can be

The Gloucester Light Infantry building where the ghost of a young lad is seen. *Photo by Arlene Nicholson.*

seen walking the village of Chepachet on occasion and has many a great tale to tell of its ghosts and history. His award-winning history lessons are worth the chat. If you see someone dressed as an early nineteenth-century soldier, it's likely Mr. Sanzi, or maybe someone from long ago still wandering the historic street. Chepachet is full of surprises.

CADY'S TAVERN

Rhode Island's Original Roadhouse

Cady's Tavern in West Glocester, Rhode Island, has been a town landmark since 1810. Hezekiah Cady opened the stagecoach stop as a resting place for travelers along the Putnam/Providence Pike. Horses were changed while the driver and passengers refreshed themselves with food and drink. Sometime during the 1920s, a fire destroyed the building, and the enterprise moved across the street. The remains of the original structure can be seen in the woods across from the present Cady's, which was once the stables and barn.

The present tavern boasts live entertainment, a friendly atmosphere, a full bar, a pub fare menu and a few resident ghosts. Such incidents include chairs and dishes being thrown by an unseen entity, voices coming from the rooms upstairs, the ghost of a little boy in the ballroom and a host of other strange events that cannot be readily explained. Recently, one of the cooks was in the kitchen preparing a meal when all the pans flew off the shelf at once. Owner Robin Tyo stated that such incidents are common in the old tavern.

In 2009, Robin inquired about having her newly purchased establishment checked out for the possibility of it being haunted. A morning visit was necessary, as the establishment opened for business at noon. There were several recent reports of ghosts in the building sighted in various areas. One of the more frequent reports was of the spirit of a child giggling and opening the door to the ballroom that sits on the second floor. His ghost was seen a few times by some of the staff and patrons. At that time, the ballroom was relegated to storage, but it once flowed with music and dance of a bygone era.

Bob and Vickie Hughes accepted the invite and invited us to come along. During a vigil, it was asked if the child would open the door. A few moments later, the latch on the door wiggled, and the door slowly creaked open. At the same time, the recorder captured a small child's voice giggling

Cady's Tavern in West Glocester. *Courtesy of Cady's Tavern.*

just after the door opened. While in the ballroom, the two got the feeling like someone was in there with them. A few more questions were asked of the little boy, to no avail. It was jokingly concluded that when the door was opened, he might have made his way out of the room and down the stairs.

The second floor used to be an apartment but was slated to become a special sitting area for those who want to escape the downstairs hustle and bustle for a few moments. In that area, the voice of a male adult and one of a female adult was captured on the recorder.

Some old photographs and newspaper clippings of the building are neatly preserved in a folder for all to peruse upon request. There is also an old signboard in the ballroom from years ago that mentions the tavern as being established in 1810. Patrons visiting the upstairs rooms have heard that date whispered in the air when inquiring how old the place was.

Cady's is known as Rhode Island's original roadhouse and rightly so. With live entertainment, open microphone nights, blues jams and great food, it is no wonder the ghosts stick around.

Tavern on Main

Of all the places in the Blackstone Valley, none is host to as much paranormal activity as the Tavern on Main in Chepachet Center.

The tavern was built in 1760 as a private home. It became a business establishment in 1799 when Cyrus Cooke turned it into a tavern and inn. In the early days of America, laws were enacted requiring a tavern or rest stop to be situated every five miles along the main thoroughfares. Most people traveled by foot, as few had horses. Cooke's tavern served as a stage stop along the Putnam Pike (Route 44) from Providence, Rhode Island, to Hartford, Connecticut. Travelers dined and lodged while fresh horses were exchanged for the next leg of the route. The food at the tavern is next to none, as it has been through the centuries. This great cuisine, coupled with its antique furnishing, makes an irresistible atmosphere for all, including those who remain long after their mortal frames have turned to dust.

The tavern first gained its notoriety when a peddler named Acote came to the inn to sell his wares. He checked in for the night, but he would never leave. For the next morning, Acote was found murdered on the back steps of the tavern. He was buried east of the inn on a hill that now bears his name.

The tavern was also the focus of one of Rhode Island's most controversial political battles. In 1842, when Thomas Dorr, the newly elected governor of Rhode Island under the People's Party, attempted to take his seat, the incumbent governor, Samuel King, refused to step down. A rebellion ensued, and King's troops marched toward the awaiting Dorr army encamped on

The Tavern on Main at the turn of the twentieth century. *From Thomas D'Agostino's private collection.*

Present view of the Tavern on Main in Chepachet. It is arguably the most haunted place in the Blackstone Valley. *Photo by Arlene Nicholson.*

Acote's Hill in Chepachet. When Dorr saw he was vastly outnumbered, he dispersed his troops and fled to nearby Connecticut. Some of Dorr's men set up a defensive in the tavern that also served as Dorr's headquarters during his endeavor to become governor. (It was his wish to have all freemen earn the right to vote, as only landowners could vote at the time.) King's troops rallied at the windows of the building, guns drawn, ready to fire, while Dorr's men stood inside with guns drawn on King's men. Jedediah Sprague jumped through a window and managed to prevent the impending skirmish. The only casualty from the rebellion took place inside the tavern when one of King's troops fired a shot through the keyhole of the door, hitting one Horace Bordeen (Bardeen) in the thigh. King's troops lodged at the tavern for the summer, nearly bankrupting the owner, Jedediah Sprague, as he was never compensated by the state for their gluttonous leisure.

H.P. Lovecraft indicated in his letters that he regularly sojourned at the tavern during his journeys to Pascoag and West Glocester's Dark Swamp in search of a creature called IT. As time rolled on, the tavern took on many roles—boardinghouse, offices and a billiards hall to name a few. There was a period in the mid- to late twentieth century where the establishment acquired a seedy reputation, as fights and other violence became a commonplace within its walls. This period may have left some scars on the atmosphere of the building that linger to this day.

The ghosts of the tavern include a woman seen in the rear left booth of the dining room; a man thought to be Thomas Dorr; another woman who is either sad or angry, or both; a few former employees and owners; and a child seen everywhere in the establishment. The countless occurrences of paranormal activity in the tavern both in the past and present could fill the pages of a book alone. Presented here are some of the most noteworthy.

There is the ghost of a woman occasionally seen in the rear corner booth of the dining room by staff and patrons alike. They used to address her as Mary Elizabeth, but subsequent EVP recordings have revealed her name to be Alice. (EVP is an abbreviation of electronic voice phenomena. This is, in short, a method of recording the voices of spirits.) Gene Waterman owned the tavern from 1982 until he retired from the business in 2004. He experienced a lot of unexplainable phenomena during his tenure as tavern keeper. Alice made her presence known to Gene numerous times. He described her as wearing colonial attire, as if she was "dressed for a picnic or a party," while she appeared to be waiting for someone to join her.

Tavern dining room. Bench in the corner is where the ghost of Alice is seen and table to the left is where the ghost of someone was caught on camera. *Photo by Arlene Nicholson.*

Another spirit is that of a little boy who is seen and heard in every room of the restaurant. One afternoon, an employee of the gas station next door and his wife witnessed the little boy looking out of the taproom window. The wife approached the window to see why a child would be in the taproom at that hour. As she neared the window, the figure backed away from the glass and vanished into the darkness. The strangest part of this account was that the tavern had been vacant and locked up during the time of the sighting.

On one occasion, a tavern keeper entered the building, as was his usual routine, at about 11:30 a.m. When he went to turn the lights on in the dining room, he saw a young boy standing just outside the ladies' room. Astonished that someone left a child there overnight, he quickly asked the boy if he was all right. The boy then turned and walked through the wall next to the kitchen door.

A father and daughter dining at the tavern met the little boy. The little girl had to use the restroom, and when she did not return after a few minutes, the father became concerned. When he approached the door, he heard his daughter talking to someone in the ladies' room. He knocked on the door and inquired how she was. She answered she was OK and was "just talking to the little boy."

Thinking it improper for a little boy to be in the bathroom, the father opened the door. His daughter was standing in front of the sink, motioning to her side where she said the boy was. She also stated that he wanted to come home with them. The father took their dinner to go and left the building in a hurry.

A woman taking an early lunch entered the dining room and proceeded toward the old coal stove where the daily soup and bread is laid out for customers to enjoy. As she approached the stove, she saw a boy standing in front of it. Thinking it was the child of an employee, she began to converse with the lad. As she spoke to him, the boy faded away in front of her.

During a dinner event at the tavern, someone decided to try an EVP session. The inquirer asked the boy, "Did you fall?" When reviewed, there was a voice of a child answering, "Did fall," followed by several seconds of giggling.

Although the ghost of the young child has been seen and heard on various occasions, the identity of the lad remains a mystery.

Dave and Kristen Lumnah took the helm of the tavern in early 2007. Since then, the ghostly occurrences have increased to the point where there is a new story to tell every week. The frequency of bizarre incidents has made the tavern arguably the most haunted place in the region.

One year, Dave asked the staff members of Brown and Hopkins, Liz and Barbara, to decorate the tavern for the season. The two were upstairs hanging red, white and blue bunting on the walls. Barbara was up on a ladder arranging one swath under a portrait, and Liz was in the opposite corner of the room doing the same. Liz suddenly heard Barbara say, "Oh no, it's all set. I got it."

Liz then asked what she needed, and Barbara, realizing that Liz was on the other side of the room, screamed, "Oh my God! I just felt somebody push my arm! I thought it was you trying to help me!"

Debra Marks, a longtime employee of the tavern, has had many experiences ranging from water turning on in the bathroom by itself to having her name called while alone in the taproom. She and her sister Chris are well acquainted with the spirits of the tavern. Chris remembers one recent incident regarding a television that sat over the end of the bar. One evening, a regular was standing below the television, stating in front of a full bar that he did not believe the tavern was haunted and the stories were all bunk. Suddenly, everyone began shouting at him to move, as the television lifted off its perch. Luckily, he was quick enough to avoid being hit as it crashed to the floor. When called in to investigate, close inspection

An unexplained light appeared at the bar in the taproom of the Tavern on Main. It could not be reproduced with further experimentation. *Courtesy of Tavern on Main.*

Area in taproom of Tavern on Main where the ghost of a little boy is often seen. *Photo by Arlene Nicholson.*

revealed that the dust on the shelf had not been disturbed, meaning that the television was actually lifted from its resting place and did not slide off the shelf. The unit suffered some case cracks but still worked fine. As for the skeptic, he was instantly converted.

The ghosts are otherwise harmless but love attention. They have tossed ketchup bottles off the shelves in front of full-capacity dinner crowds, lifted tablecloths before astonished eyes and pinched a waiter. A former bartender was alone one night preparing the coolers for the next day. He went into the basement to bring up the supplies needed before placing them on the floor next to the bar. He opened the coolers to see what bays were to be refilled but was interrupted by a strange noise. Peering over the bar, he noticed one of the beer bottles was out of the case and spinning like a top on the floor. He decided it was time to lock up and worry about the rest in the morning. These are just a few of the accounts and experiences at the Tavern on Main.

The ghosts of the tavern vary in era and personality. They are the remnants of those who either passed through town or had made the building an essential part of their lives. From the little boy to the woman in the rear booth and the other restless spirits, all seem to be attracted to the people who come to the tavern to wine and dine. Perhaps they are just attempting to mingle with the patrons or have something they wish to relate. The energy in the tavern is strong, intense, yet pleasing, making it the perfect place for a haunting. The website www.tavernonmainri.com even has a video taken during one of our investigations in 2006. The video was captured on a young investigator's camera, and although we tried to re-create it numerous times, we have yet to explain what we captured. We can only surmise at this point that it was someone from long ago still biding time at the tavern.

LINCOLN

SAYLESVILLE MILL

William Sayles and his son, Frank, established the village of Saylesville in the mid-nineteenth century. William established a bleachery, located between Scott Pond, Barney Pond and Bleachery Pond. When William died, his son took over the business. By the time Frank died in 1920, the Sayles Mill was one of the largest textile-finishing enterprises in the world. The forty-acre complex employed three thousand workers, turning out seventy-five million yards of cotton goods each year. Although the factory was one of the largest in the region, it became more renowned for an incident that took place in 1934.

The largest strike in American history took place on Labor Day of that year. Some 400,000 workers from New England to the South walked off the job and took to the picket lines. Several thousand factory workers and sympathizers picketed the Saylesville Mill, then known as Manville Jenkes Company.

Workers outside the mill protested for union representation and fair wages while those within the mill held fast for days for fear of losing their jobs and, even more, their lives. When the mob became unruly, owners of the mill called on Governor Greene to send some assistance. The National Guard showed up with machine guns and gas grenades in hopes of suppressing the growing unrest.

The mob charged after the guard, which opened fire on the crowd. Hundreds dispersed into the Moshassuck Cemetery, where they continued to pelt the guardsmen with stones, sticks and other projectiles. In the end, 4 workers and 8 sympathizers lay dead, with 132 others injured in the melee. The first casualty of the skirmish was Charles Gorczynski, a seventeen-year-old laborer from Central Falls.

The event came to be known as the Saylesville Massacre. A monument dedicated to the tragedy sits in the Moshassuck Cemetery as well as a gravestone with two bullet holes from a guardsman's machine gun.

Such an event is not without its mark on the delicate fabric of this world. The spirits of those who lost their lives still wander the area where the struggle took place. Among them are more recent entities that were perhaps caught in the energy that has lingered on the grounds for so long. Deborah Vickers had this story to share regarding her experience at the mill:

> *Our friend Cindy reported that her boyfriend worked at the Saylesville Mills, which are at the end of our street. His boss owned a moving company and rented out storage spaces in the mill. He would occasionally hear his name*

Memorial to the four workers killed during the 1934 labor strike at the Saylesville Mill. *Photo by Kelly Pincins.*

Gravestone in the Moshassuck Cemetery with two bullet holes from the Saylesville Massacre of 1934. *Photo by Kelly Pincins.*

called when no one else was there and often heard footsteps when he knew the mill was otherwise vacant. Some of the workers refused to go into certain sections of the mill because of the strange activity that they experienced while in those areas.

Cindy asked Deb if she would like to check things out after a lessee of one of the storage units passed away. Unexplainable activity began taking place shortly after the renter died. Footsteps, voices and noises pervaded the area as if someone was still using the unit. Deb brought her daughters and some recorders to see what they could find. Deb asked a series of questions while her daughters rummaged through the items strewn about the locker. Later, when they listened to their recorder, they were astonished to find several instances where an ethereal voice spoke. When Deb asked how the person died, a voice was heard saying, "the liver."

Other answers concluded that the person's name was Nicholas, and he was a drag queen known as "Carisse" on stage. Among the items found in the unit was a box of dressmaking patterns that were part of Nicholas's original creations. One of the statements on the recorder that took Deb by surprise was "She found the patterns."

Deb felt it was important to Nicholas that someone would find the patterns and perhaps give them a new life. She gave them to a friend, a seamstress, hoping it would bring Nicholas some peace.

The owners of the mill decided to renovate and removed the storage units. Deb returned when they were clearing everything out. The energy she felt was different from the first time she visited the building. She did report, however, that during the move, she felt someone touch her head when no one was nearby, making her question if there are still other spirits still lingering in the mill that have yet to communicate with this side of the veil.

THE HEARTHSIDE HOUSE

Interestingly enough, the Hearthside House (b. 1810) on Great Road is known as "The House that Love Built," and to this day, that moniker stands true. The history of Hearthside is compelling, but to have an extraordinary energy within its walls only adds to the wonder and mystique the building exudes.

With a commanding presence along this historic roadway, Hearthside stands two and a half stories high, is made entirely of stone and features a gable roof rising up to impressive ogee curves trimmed out with a beaded cornice. Granite lintels top the windows, and tall wooden pillars hold the full-height front portico, reminiscent of Mount Vernon. The portico is topped by a dormer, which repeats the curve of the roof and beaded cornice. The main entrance has a six-paneled door, with double pilasters on each side, enclosed side lighting and crowned by an elliptical fanlight. Upon entering the front door into the elegant foyer, visitors are greeted by a graceful flying staircase, with stairs set in a counter-clockwise direction around a Tuscan column. It was thought that either the builder was left-handed or if intruders were to enter the home, the owner had the upper hand with his sword for defense over the stair railings. There are ten rooms, with a fireplace in each room, plus a third-floor attic and another attic space above. There are some special rarities the Hearthside boasts—among them is a Rumford oven found in 2002 when a crack in the dining room wall was opened for repair. The oven was installed around the 1820s or '30s and was the latest innovation in cooking at the time. There are only a few of these ancient "modern" conveniences left intact in the United States, making it a must-see for fanciers of history.

The Hearthside in Lincoln is well worth a visit. *From Thomas D'Agostino's private collection.*

Another rare gem is the Pipes of Pan hidden within the front parlor fireplace. When a fire burned in the hearth, a knob on the mantel would open up a mechanism that would allow air to enter, causing a flute-like sound. In 2009, the Friends of Hearthside received a grant to make necessary repairs to the chimney and to investigate what this mechanism was and how it worked. The findings showed a crevice with a metal paddle attached to a rod leading to the knob on the front of the fireplace. While testing was done with several fires in the fireplace, the sound could not be replicated, as the pipe providing the wind necessary to initiate the instrument had been long sealed. The fireplace was converted to gas for safety reasons, so the pipes remain silent for now. Research showed that although these may have been common in castles around Europe, this example is the only one in this country.

Stephen Hopkins Smith was in his twenties when he built Hearthside. The Smiths, who were Quakers and farmers, lived in a stone-ender house on 249 acres surrounding the area where Hearthside was eventually built. Stephen's grandmother Anne Smith was the granddaughter of John Smith, the miller, and one of five who crossed the Seekonk River with Roger Williams on his first landing in Providence. According to popular folklore, Stephen Hopkins Smith won $40,000 in a lottery. He used his winnings to construct a house exceptional enough to win the heart of a young socialite from Providence, who had informed him that she must live in one of the grandest homes in the state. When the mansion was completed, Smith took his beloved for a buggy ride along the Great Road. His plan was to bring her to the magnificent home he had built for her. When she gazed upon it with astonishment, he would then declare it was built for her. The two would then settle down in the home that love built. Unfortunately, the trip did not turn out as planned. Upon approaching Hearthside, the young lady exclaimed, "My, what a beautiful house, but who would ever want to live way out here in the wilderness?" Those very words were enough to break Smith's heart. He brought her back to Providence, never married and never lived in the house. He instead moved into a small cottage nearby. Because of this sad legend, Hearthside has sometimes been referred to as Heartbreak House or, better still, the House that Love Built.

Stephen also constructed a stone textile mill and started the Smith Manufacturing Company, later called the Butterfly Mill. Unfortunately, his textile business proved unprofitable. Smith died in 1857 at the age of seventy-four and is buried in the cemetery at the Saylesville Friends Meeting House a short distance away from Hearthside on Great Road.

Simon Eddy Thornton became the owner of the house in 1870. He remained there until his death on May 2, 1873. His body was prepared at the home by the undertaker, who came with his equipment and a portable embalming table. The coffin was displayed in the drawing room, where visitors would come and pay their respects. Following the ceremony, the coffin was carried out of the house and into a waiting hearse to bring it to the gravesite for burial.

Each October, Hearthside, along with its volunteers, gets draped in black, giving all who pass by the message that this is a house in mourning. It is a re-creation of the Victorian mourning customs practiced in the era Simon Thornton passed away, with displays in each room of the house, including mourning clothing, jewelry, artwork, stationery displays, postmortem photography and other funerary exhibits. A mock funeral ceremony was featured to kick off the 2012 event, complete with an 1868 hearse. During the exhibit, the Hearthside hosts special programs such as having a medium and tarot card readers, typical of the times to comfort the mourners in assuring them that their loved ones had passed safely into the light.

One note of interest, Simon Thornton's sister was Alzada Smith Thornton Chase, wife of Benjamin Chase, the original owner of the neighboring Chase Farm and the great-great-grandfather of Kathy Chase Hartley, the

Victorian funeral re-creation is always a must at the Hearthside. *Photo by Arlene Nicholson.*

founder of the Friends of Hearthside, making Simon Thornton her great-great uncle.

Daniel Meader was the next to own the Hearthside, purchasing it in 1890 after he retired from farming. Frederick Clark Sayles acquired the home in 1901, having bought the surrounding farmland and the Butterfly Mill several years earlier. Sayles made substantial improvements to the farm, which he named Mariposa (later called the Butterfly Farm). Frederick Sayles was also known for being the first mayor of Pawtucket, Rhode Island, in 1885. The Sayles brothers owned one of the world's largest mills, the Sayles Bleachery, and were generous donors to their community. The area around the mills became known as Saylesville, the village in Lincoln where Hearthside is located.

Arnold Gindrat Talbot purchased the house in 1904 as both a home and a site for the family's hand weaving business known as the Hearthside Looms. This is how the Hearthside got its name. Together with his wife, Katharine, and their two children, William and Frances, as well as weavers from Portugal, Talbot created a variety of fabrics using historical patterns and produced fine linens, bedspreads, tablecloths and rugs.

The last family to call Hearthside their home was Andrew and Penelope Mowbray and their three children, Andrew, Sherry and Stuart. The Mowbrays purchased the house and one acre of land in 1956 and lived here for forty years, longer than any other residents. Andrew was responsible for nominating Hearthside for placement in the National Register of Historic Places in 1972. Mowbray was an avid collector, especially of military memorabilia, and his extensive collection of antiques, guns and swords filled the house. Mowbray also owned several antique cars; many of them were early models of the Rolls-Royce. One of his cars saw use in *The Great Gatsby* (1974), filmed in Newport, Rhode Island. Mowbray was not too happy about letting someone else drive his prized possession, so he played a chauffeur in the movie. In 1976, he published *The American Rolls-Royce, A Comprehensive History of Rolls-Royce of America, Inc.* Penelope Mowbray had a collection of antique doorknockers she started as a child in the hopes that she would someday have a home in which to display them.

Her dream came true when she and Andrew purchased Hearthside, and today the house boasts these fine trinkets on the doors. In fact, after she had left home, she returned to finish what she started, acquiring more doorknockers, eventually adorning every door in the mansion with one. She also had a home-based business selling Betsy Ross flags and was actively involved in efforts to preserve Great Road's historic character. To ensure that Hearthside would be protected in the future, the Mowbray family sold the house to the Town of Lincoln in 1996 when Andrew passed away. Under the leadership of lifelong town resident Kathy Hartley, a group of dedicated citizens formed the all-volunteer organization, Friends of Hearthside Inc., in 2001 to serve as stewards and open the mansion to the public.

With all this history, many ask if the Hearthside still holds the revenants of those who lived within its walls. Some have hinted that they have experienced strange feelings in one room or another or heard noises while alone in the house. The volunteers have collected several photographs of what appear to be spirits mingling with guests on tours over the years. During the Victorian funeral exhibit in 2014, a photographer captured a most interesting photo as he pointed his camera at the front of the house in the darkness of night. In the photo, there is an image of a full body of a man dressed in old-fashioned clothing floating outside the second-floor window peering into the room where the body of Simon Thornton had been prepared for burial. The guests who attend this exhibit never know who will be hosting a card reading or trying to communicate with Mr. Thornton or other former residents. In each case, the featured guest

Picture taken at the window of the room where Victorian funeral re-creation was on display at the Hearthside. That is not an actor. *Courtesy of the Hearthside House.*

presenter delves into the unseen energies in the Hearthside, providing us with even more information to ponder its history.

There is undoubtedly a strong energy to the Hearthside, and it is one of love and peace, which seems to be experienced by all who pass through its impressive entranceway. The people who volunteer their time, guests who tour the place and even a writer for *Yankee Magazine* have felt the same intense feeling that makes the place magical. For what it's worth, a place does not have to have ghosts inhabiting its rooms to be haunted. The *haunt* might just be a very strong feeling that encompasses its perimeter. In the case of the Hearthside, it is the haunt called love.

NORTH SMITHFIELD

A VAMPIRE'S DEADLY GRASP

New England is known as the vampire capital of the world, yet many New Englanders are not aware of that fact. From a documented Connecticut case in 1784 until Mercy Brown of Exeter's 1892 exorcism for a belief that she may have been one of the undead, historians and researchers have uncovered many cases of suspected vampirism in the annals of New England. Town records, histories, newspaper articles and other publications bring to light the darker side of New England's past. Although we may have these crumbling documents to read as proof the people of the region feared vampires in the form of a spectral ghoul lurked among them, North Smithfield has a case written in stone, literally.

Just shy of the North Smithfield–Woonsocket border is the Union Cemetery Annex on Smithfield Road. The more modern cemetery is bordered on its eastern edge by several smaller burial lots that were in existence long before the larger grounds became a place of eternal repose. Among those smaller lots, covered in brush and saplings, is the grave of Simon Whipple Aldrich. Simon was the youngest son of Colonel Dexter and Margery Aldrich, and he died of consumption on May 6, 1841, at twenty-seven years of age.

Simon Whipple Aldrich was one of several family members who died at a relatively young age. His elder sister died shortly before him, and his younger sister died three years after. In fact, several of the children died at

Simon Whipple Aldrich's stone. Note the epitaph on the bottom of the stone. *Photo by Arlene Nicholson.*

fairly young ages: Polly (1801–August 13, 1825), Patience (1808–December 12, 1831), Anna (1818–May 14, 1842) and Betsey (1828–May 12, 1844). Although consumption might be to blame, there is no record of any family members that might have been exhumed and exorcised as suspected vampires, which was a real fear at the time. The interesting aspect of this account is what is carved in Simon Whipple Aldrich's stone. It reads:

> *In Memory of Simon Whipple Youngest son of Col. Dexter Aldrich & Margery his wife who died May 6, 1841 aged 27 years.*

The inscription below reads,

> *Altho consumption's vampire grasp had seized thy mortal frame…ing mind.*

The bottom of the stone has been cemented into the base, covering the rest of the inscription, which may have consisted of two or more lines, but the upper portion is quite revealing in the way the two words are paired together. Did the Aldrich family believe a vampire was at work, or was it just a metaphorical way of saying that the dreaded disease was a microscopic vampire that sucked the life out of their loved ones? If you visit the Union Cemetery, take a moment to wander down the leftmost road, and you will see a well-worn path leading to the grave that has carved in stone a case of "consumption's vampire grasp."

One incident worth mentioning was a visit to the grave by Arlene Nicholson to shoot photographs. She had a recorder with her and decided to try to communicate with the spirit of Simon. She asked a few questions, including, "Simon, where are you now?" When she played the recorder, she heard an answer, "Right beside you." At that time, she was standing with the gravestone to her left.

PAWTUCKET

GHOSTS OF THE INDUSTRIAL REVOLUTION

Slater Mill

Blackstone Valley may have been named for its first white settler, Reverend William Blackstone (Blaxton), but it was another man who came much later that would change the tide of the region forever. In 1793, Samuel Slater became the catalyst for the Industrial Revolution in America. Slater was born in Derbyshire, England, on June 9, 1768. At an early age, he started working as an apprentice in a nearby cotton mill. Slater learned everything he could about the mill machines and their design. Rising to superintendent was not enough for the young man with big plans. Slater wanted to build his fortune in the newly formed United States of America.

The only setback was a British law that strictly forbade textile workers to leave the country with any such plans or documents pertaining to the construction of the machines, so Slater instead memorized the components and set out for America in 1789 to find his fortune.

The machines, built by Richard Arkwright, were the latest innovations of the times. Moses Brown, a Quaker merchant, had confidence in the young man and helped fund the enterprise. By 1791, a water wheel textile factory under the leadership of Samuel Slater and several other partners turned machinery that spun wool and cotton into thread, and the

Slater Mill Site in Pawtucket is home to several ghosts. *From Thomas D'Agostino's private collection.*

American Industrial Revolution was born. In 1793, the wooden Yellow Mill was erected and became the first successful cotton-spinning factory in the United States. In keeping with the American Dream, the mill officially opened on July 4, 1793.

Samuel Slater may have been considered a spy because of the way he smuggled precious information out of Great Britain, but to the United States, he was the father of industry. It may be true that he employed children to work in his factory, but they were treated fairly and whole families lived and worked on the grounds of the mill site. In 1803, Slater and his brother expanded the model, creating a factory and village—in present-day North Smithfield—known as Slatersville. The factory village included housing, a company store, a bank, meeting places and a post office. These little ready-made villages sprang up all over New England, especially the Blackstone Valley, and became known as the Rhode Island System.

Before long, the Blackstone River and its tributaries were laced with mills of all forms of manufacture. Villages sprouted out of nowhere, and people flocked to work at the mills in hopes of a better life. Children were more often than not employed at the more rural mills because many adults felt that such work was beneath their stature. Their farms were of the utmost importance, but as much as they reaped, money was still a necessity and children could work the mills to help with the family finances while the adults kept house with the daily chores. Another reason mill owners preferred the young folk was because child labor was cheap, and children could fit easily between and under the machines to fix any problems that arose.

Slater was fair and sensitive to the families he employed. He set up a four-part system of factory work that children of ages four to ten could easily perform. But not all mill owners were as conscientious as Slater. Early mills were hazardous places to work, and many employees either lost their lives or were permanently maimed by the merciless machines they were hired to operate. The tragic accidents in these factories have left the interiors of these buildings scarred with the spirits of those who gave their hard labor, sweat and blood to the place they would forever haunt. Slater Mill, Samuel's first venture, in Pawtucket, Rhode Island, is no exception. In fact, Slater Mill is one of the most haunted mills of the Blackstone Valley.

The Slater Mill Historical Complex consists of Slater Mill, Wilkinson Mill and the Sylvanus Brown House. All three buildings are haunted. The main mill, Slater Mill, produced various goods for over two centuries, including coffin trimmings, tools for the jewelry industry and cardboard, until finally closing its doors in 1921. The mill was purchased for its prominence as the birthplace of the Industrial Revolution, and investors—including Henry Ford, Walter Chrysler and Harvey Firestone—turned the decaying structure into a living museum. From 1925 to the early 1950s, the museum was open by appointment. Since then, it has been open on a regular basis for tours and other special events. It is the spirits of the mill that keep the wonder of its history alive, and they are not shy about showing themselves.

Carl and Keith Johnson, docents of Slater Mill, have witnessed many strange occurrences during their tenure at the site. On October 26, 2016, Carl took us on a tour of the three buildings, telling stories of the haunting. The Slater Mill building contains the ghosts of a boy and a man, perhaps Samuel Slater, founder of the mill. The weaving machine, on loan from Great Britain, is the focal point for the ghost of the boy, who may have lost his life trying to dodge the carrier as it came by while he would have been repairing the thread on one of the spindles.

During our tour, Carl explained that one of his previous tour groups heard the scream of a child while in front of the weaving machine. He ran behind the machine thinking a child on the tour got caught up in something, but there was no one there.

Carl began demonstrating to us how the children would have to run behind the weaving machine to reattach broken threads while the carrier was still moving. He explained in detail how the child would reattach the thread and then quickly drop to the floor as the carrier rolled by above them.

They would then make sure the carrier was clear before jumping up and out of the way before it returned. All the while, his presentation was being recorded. When the recorder was played back, instead of our three voices, there were five. In one segment of the recording, we interjected: "So you and someone else actually heard the child scream?" A voice of a woman can be heard saying, "They were two six-year-olds." Shortly after, a man's voice was heard saying, "They did not have a prayer."

Several visitors have witnessed the ghost of a man on the stairs leading to the second floor. Upon inspection, both the stairs and the second floor were vacant of any such person.

On October 29, 2016, the mill hosted a public investigation to celebrate the Halloween season along with the ghosts of the site. During one of the vigils, Keith started the dangerous weaving machine to show the group how it works. After all was quiet, someone asked, "Did you make it out alright? You don't look like you were hurt." A few moments later everyone heard what sounded like a long, painful moan of a child coming from inside the room. The ghostly scream was recorded on several units that were running at the time of the incident.

On several occasions, the sudden and unexplained starting of a machine on its own volition has frightened staff and visitors. Such an occurrence is no small feat, as the power must first be turned on before turning the safety switches that bring the primitive machinery to life.

A man named Albert E. Jackson attempted to cross the river at the milldam on December 21, 1907, the date of the winter solstice. Unfortunately, he lost his footing and drowned. His body was found the next day with one leg wedged between a boulder and the side of the dam abutments. The Slater Mill Preservation Society decided to hold a special public investigation on December 21 as a celebration to usher in the coming of winter. While in the mill, the investigators heard a voice upstairs shouting, "Hello, hello." Two parties ran up the only staircase leading to where the voice was heard. As they reached the top of the stairs, they were met with an eerie silence. The second story was void of any other living person. Could it have been Mr. Jackson? Was he in the mill on December 21, 1907, searching for someone before he attempted to cross the river? These questions remain unanswered, as do the actual identities of the eternal inhabitants of Slater Mill.

The Sylvanus Brown House is home to a little girl the staff calls Becca. Becca has been heard giggling and speaking on many occasions. She has also been observed peering out the top-story windows. The sightings of her go back as far as people can remember. In the early 1990s, a mother and her daughter decided to take a tour of the complex. While basking in the garden at the rear of the Brown house, the daughter felt someone was watching her and happened to glance up at the windows, where she noticed a young girl staring back. The figure then moved from one window to the next before disappearing into thin air. She quickly asked the tour guide who was in the home. The guide told her the home was still locked but would soon be opened for the tour, and there was no one else with her on the complex grounds at the time. When the startled young woman mentioned her incident, she and her mother got more than they bargained for in the telling of the young girl's ghost who still resides in the Brown house.

During several tours, the spirit of Becca has addressed the guests. In one case, a guest entered the bedroom only to hear a voice say, "Hey, get out of here."

In the basement of the house there is a kitchen with two fireplaces; the room is set up for exhibition purposes with fireplaces, table and pantry made to appear as if meals are about to be served. Several years ago, a group of Girl Scouts took a tour with Carl as their guide. He recounted that a few of the girls sat on a bench in front of one of the fireplaces. Apparently, the spirits of the home did not care for this act. The bench, with the girls on it, slid two feet from its original position into the middle of the floor.

The Wilkinson Mill was built between 1810 and 1811 by Oziel Wilkinson, whose daughter Hannah married Samuel Slater. Oziel's son David was a mechanical genius at a very young age. It was David who built much of the machinery and tooling for the mills, thus setting in motion a dynasty and close relationship between the Wilkinsons and Slaters that would carry on for many years to come. Both families built mills in various parts of New England, including Connecticut and Massachusetts. David's work with steam power was renowned throughout the region. His first steam-powered boat was successfully tested on the Providence River in 1793—fourteen years before Robert Fulton's steamship, *Clermont*, took sail. In fact, Fulton's engineer, Daniel French, came to Rhode Island to see the monumental occasion. In his later years, David Wilkinson did not refer to Fulton as an inventor, but as "simply a busy collector of other people's inventions."

The wheel pit of the Wilkinson Mill is home to a man who reportedly got caught in the wheel and died. Many people have experienced anxious feelings while in the wheel pit. Visitors have felt something touch them or brush against them when no one was otherwise in the area. During a tour, a woman had her hair tugged in front of a group of people. Her head snapping back, as her hair was pulled outward, was noticeable to everyone in the room.

There is a rumor that a small boy was killed in the room when he got caught in the wheel gears. This death has never been substantiated, and it is unlikely that a young lad would have been charged to perform anything in the wheel area. Adult strength was necessary for all tasks involving the starting, stopping and maintenance of the great wheel that ran the mill.

In the mill itself, people have seen a dark figure moving about the far end of the main floor. Carl Johnson and another investigator were standing on the far end of the mill near the entrance when they both witnessed a dark misty figure walk to the center of the room and stop, as if noticing them. Both witnesses stared at the figure, which then moved toward the machinery, vanishing among spindles and drive belts.

A tour of the mill is in itself an education. The wheel, now powered by electricity, turns all the belts that run the machines the same as it did when powered by water. It is impressive to witness firsthand the ingenuity of manufacturing in early America. It is also amazing how some of these manufacturers have stayed behind, lingering forever in living history.

PROVIDENCE

ROGER WILLIAMS

William Blackstone may have been the first white settler to establish a home in what is now the state of Rhode Island, but it was Roger Williams who established a colony that would become the first known settlement in the state. In 1636, Williams and a few of his faithful followers left Massachusetts Bay Colony to forge a settlement in the wilderness. The Puritan doctrine was much too strict for these pioneers, who wished to practice freedom of religion, and they set out to forge their own religious colony. The group settled on a hill in what is now known as Providence and began to build their homes. They traded with the local Indian tribes, and as time passed, Williams built a trading post in South County where he could barter with the local tribes. Reverend William Blackstone, along with others, would often visit these locales to preach the word of God. What a sight it must have been to see the white-haired and bearded Blackstone meandering along the trail on his beloved bull.

Williams learned much of the Indian language and was considered a scholar of their ways. More and more people of various religious persuasions began to flock to what was now the Providence Plantation. Williams and his wife, Mary, had six children. He died in 1683 at the age of eighty years and was buried in his backyard. In 1860, it was decided that the founder of the State of Rhode Island should be interred in a

The Roger Williams Memorial, where the scant remains of Rhode Island's founder are buried. *Photo by Arlene Nicholson.*

more suitable place of recognition, so his body was exhumed. Much to the surprise of those in attendance, there was more than they had bargained for.

Among the remains were nails, teeth and bone fragments, all expected to be what was left of him, but something else had taken place over the centuries. An apple tree had turned Williams's remains into a root. The root had entered the coffin, curving down Williams's head and entering the chest cavity. It then split at the legs and turned upward into the feet.

The remains of nails, teeth and bone fragments were reburied in the Old North Burial Ground until 1936, when they were once again exhumed and buried under the statue of Williams at Prospect Terrace. The statue at 188 Pratt Street sits across from the lot that Williams's house once graced. The root is on display in the Brown Museum Carriage House inside a coffin-shaped frame protected by a wire screen.

So an apple tree that many people likely ate from ended up eating the founder of Rhode Island. If this is the case, then there are people who unknowingly have some of Roger Williams's blood in their family roots.

The man never stood for a portrait or had a statue of him made while he was alive. All subsequent images of him are from the artist's impression of his probable likeness. It seems nature has preserved the closest image we have of the founder of Rhode Island. (Legend has it that it was a Sprague who planted the apple tree at the head of Roger Williams' first gravesite.)

BENEFIT STREET

Benefit Street, initially known as Back Street, cut along the back of Providence. Originally, religious leader Roger Williams formed the colony after being ousted from the Plymouth Colony for his liberal beliefs in religious practices. In time, more people joined his way of thinking, and the colony grew and flourished to the point where it became a city. As prominent people took to this new city, they chose the hill overlooking the Providence River, where the less affluent could look up at the grand homes as one might peer upward at Mount Olympus for a glimpse of the gods.

By 1770, it became necessary to widen the road and straighten its winding curves for ease of travel. As this would be a benefit for all who traveled it, the throughway was renamed Benefit Street. Many of the homes remain much as they did back in the eighteenth and nineteenth centuries when they were constructed. Due to the lack of a formal burial ground, Providence families buried their loved ones on their property. When renovations took place on Back Street, many of these deceased were exhumed and removed to the newly built North Burial Ground. Some are convinced that this mass exhumation became a catalyst for the ghostly activity that plagues the area. Although this may be so, several other famous people have lent their ethereal services in making Benefit Street the most haunted neighborhood in Providence.

The ghost of Edgar Allan Poe is still seen wandering Benefit Street, as his last love, Sarah Helen Whitman, resided at what is now 88 Benefit Street. Many have seen a man resembling the great writer cloaked in black, adorned with a top hat and walking stick (fashionable for Poe's time) meandering along the street late at night. He is seen approaching the doorstep of Whitman's former home and then vanishing. Poe and Whitman also haunt the Athenaeum.

Poe frequently stayed at the Mansion House Hotel during his visits to Providence. A former tenant found an old slipper belonging to a woman in the closet of his bedroom. When no one came forward to claim the lost item, he discarded it, and from that night until he vacated the property, he was roused from his sleep by the voluble sound of a Victorian skirt rustling in his room, as if someone was in search of something.

One home on the street was once a music school, and the sound of a piano is sometimes heard echoing through its chambers despite the fact that no such instrument is present in the house.

Rhode Island School of Design has buildings lacing the area, and many of them are reputedly haunted. Of course, some may be urban legends intended to scare the newcomers to the institution while others have no explanation.

Barstow House is said to house demonic entities that cause extreme cold and depression. If one is up late in the night, the vast mirrors will reflect the spirits that are reported to dwell within the house.

The Dexter House at 187 Benefit Street was once a morgue, so it is no surprise that many a ghost of those whose bodies were brought there still roam the halls of the building. The Dunnell House, although located close by on Angell Street, likewise has a few ghosts. The home's ghosts mostly confine themselves to the basement, where they like to make noise and topple items stored there. The face of an old woman has been seen peering out of a second-story window of the building by people passing by.

Benefit Street, where Edgar Allan Poe is seen walking up to the Whitman house. *Photo by Arlene Nicholson.*

Homer Hall and Farnum Hall also are home to some former tenants—in the former, a man and woman who like to break personal items and turn the water faucets on.

Two child ghosts who love to play in the basement and a woman who is seen on the second floor occupy the Pardon Miller House on Angell Street, also close to Benefit Street. Perhaps she is in eternal pursuit of the two children—they may have been hers in life but are now separated by physical walls in death.

The Nightingale-Brown House is home to perhaps the most interesting of the college haunts. This building, located at 357 Benefit Street, is owned by Brown University and is home to the John Nicholas Brown Center for Public Humanities and Cultural Heritage. It is also the permanent home to one of its previous owners, who seemed to harbor abhorrence to darkness. The Nightingale family sold the home to Nicholas Brown in 1814. The Brown family resided in the home from that time until 1985, when they gifted it to the university.

One evening, two custodians were tidying up the building. The senior custodian was upstairs, while the newly hired hand was cleaning the first floor. As the newer custodian performed his nightly task, he had the uncanny feeling that the eyes on one of the portraits in the room followed his every move. Having become a bit unnerved but happy to finish his job, the man exited the room, shutting the lights behind him. In an instant, a loud voice erupted from the chamber, "Do not turn the lights off!!!"

The frightened man raced up the stairs to where his co-worker was and frantically recounted what had just transpired. Upon hearing the story, the senior custodian calmly stated, "Yeah, we all know about the portrait and that it speaks. Just don't listen to it, and by all means, never turn the lights off in that room."

One of the most unsettling and eeriest of the Benefit Street haunts is that of the phantom carriage. One evening, a college professor decided to take a late-night stroll along the historic street. The night was agreeable, and the moon spilled a warm, welcoming light over the landscape. In a moment, something caught his eye. He turned and observed a horse-drawn carriage moving quietly down the empty street. The wheels moved, and the horse's hooves pounded the pavement; however, no sound whatsoever could be heard. The carriage silently moved down the lane and out of sight.

The professor is not the only person to have witnessed this ghostly apparition. According to legend, an eight-year-old boy named George Kelly was killed when the carriage he was riding in struck a pothole,

The Nightingale-Brown House, where a portrait prefers to have the light lit. *Photo by Arlene Nicholson.*

A view of haunted Benefit Street. *Photo by Arlene Nicholson.*

ejecting him from the vehicle and running over him. On the first crisp fall evening, the carriage silently makes its way down Benefit Street, vanishing in the night mist.

Over the years, many have witnessed the spectral carriage and horses as it parades without a sound down haunted Benefit Street.

THE GHOST OF EDGAR ALLAN POE IN PROVIDENCE

There are numerous writings about Edgar Allan Poe's tales of his travels and life. I wish to deal with his ghostly visits to Providence, as it falls neatly inside of the New England landscape.

Edgar Allan Poe was born in Boston on January 19, 1809. His journeys in his short forty-year lifespan took him to many places, including those that resided in his mind. Poe was the child of two actors. His father left when he was very young, and his mother died a year later. John and Frances Allan of Richmond, Virginia, took him in. Here he would spend his childhood and early adult years.

Poe attended the University of Virginia for a semester and even became a cadet at West Point after enlisting in the army in 1827. He reached the rank of sergeant major, the highest noncommissioned rank one could receive. Unfortunately, his writing beckoned. He began composing poems while writing for several journals and periodicals. In 1836, he married his thirteen-year-old cousin, Virginia Clemm. She died of tuberculosis on January 30, 1847. Poe had been drinking heavily due to the stress of her illness.

Shortly after Virginia's death, he started courting Sarah Helen Whitman of Providence, Rhode Island, whom he had met in July 1845. Whitman, a poet and spiritualist, was a fan of Poe's work. They would exchange letters for a period until he proposed and she accepted on the condition he would remain sober until the day of the wedding. This he promised, but the vow lasted only a few days. He began drinking again and even attempted to kill himself. Whitman supposedly received an anonymous letter while she was at the library (Providence Athenaeum) stating that Poe had broken his vow to her to stay sober, directly leading to an end of the relationship. It was in that famous building at 251 Benefit Street that Whitman officially broke off her engagement with the author on December 23, 1848. Poe was also accused of trying to woo another woman. Poe noted in a letter to Whitman addressed "Dear Madam" that he blamed her mother for their failed relationship.

An old photo of the Providence Athenaeum where Poe and Lovecraft spent hours reading. *From Thomas D'Agostino's private collection.*

On October 3, 1849, Poe was wandering the streets of Baltimore in a delirious state. He was taken to the Washington Medical College, where he died four days later. It is reported his final words were, "Lord help my poor soul."

Causes of death were speculated to be inflammation of the brain, rabies, syphilis, cholera, heart disease and meningeal inflammation, to name a few, but it remains a mystery, as the records mysteriously disappeared shortly after his death, along with his death certificate.

Poe's body may lie in repose, but his ghost still roams the area where he lived with Sarah Whitman. People have reported seeing Poe's ghost walking along Benefit Street, stopping at the home where Whitman lived. He quietly strolls by the unexpected party, who then realizes that something is very bizarre in the visage of the individual who just passed. As they turn, the man stops and looks up at them, revealing the face of Poe before vanishing into thin air at the home's doorstep.

The Providence Athenaeum was one of the couple's favorite haunts in life. It appears to be Poe's in death as well. A very strange event was recorded in the 1980s and has occasionally replayed many times since. A disheveled man was seen sleeping on the stairs of the Athenaeum late one night by a passerby. His rough and drunken appearance gave rise to the thought that

Stairs of the Athenaeum where the ghost of Edgar Allan Poe was spotted. *Photo by Arlene Nicholson.*

he was homeless and could use some aid. The passerby approached the man in an attempt to aid him in any way he could. The vagabond awoke, and with a dreary, solemn look on his face, he replied, "I was dreaming of the conqueror worm. I thank you for waking me."

Satisfied that the man was in no need of assistance, the passerby continued on, but after a few feet, he turned one more time and glanced back at the character on the stairs. At that instant, the figure became misty and slowly dissipated before his eyes. As the lights from the streets shone on the face of the poor soul, the passerby saw it was none other than the countenance of Poe himself.

Does Poe still walk the streets of Providence? Why not? It was the last place he found peace and perhaps will eternally wander and visit the buildings that hosted his once mortal frame.

Note: Each year, around the anniversary of Poe's death, Keith and Carl Johnson present a special tribute to the legendary author on the lawn of the Ladd Observatory at Doyle and Hope Streets in Providence.

LOVECRAFT AND THE LADD OBSERVATORY

It is quite amazing that two of the most revered horror writers of all time once called Providence their home. It is even more amazing that they both still haunt the city streets. Poe has his place in the Athenaeum, and Howard Phillips Lovecraft has the Ladd Observatory to hang around in, just as he did when he walked this earth in a mortal frame. Although Lovecraft, like Poe, was a regular at the Athenaeum, he seems to prefer the solitude of the observatory to make his ghostly rounds.

The Ladd Observatory opened in 1891 with generous donations from Governor Herbert Ladd. Winslow Upton, Brown University professor of astronomy, became its first director. Upton was born in Salem, Massachusetts, on October 12, 1853, and died on January 8, 1914. Upton was fond of young Lovecraft and his passion for the stars. He even gave Lovecraft a key to the observatory so he could come and go as he pleased:

The late Prof. Upton of Brown, a friend of the family, gave me the freedom of the college observatory, & I came & went there at will on my bicycle. Ladd Observatory tops a considerable eminence about a mile from the house. I used to walk up Doyle Avenue with my wheel, but when returning

Ladd Observatory in Providence, where the ghost of Lovecraft has been reported wandering the premises. *From Thomas D'Agostino's private collection.*

83

would have a glorious coast down it....I suppose I pestered the people at the observatory half to death, but they were very kind about it.

Upton may be long gone, but Lovecraft still seems to come and go as he pleases. His apparition has been witnessed on the grounds of the building, and neighbors have seen him peering out the windows of the historic structure. It seems Howard Phillips Lovecraft still clings to the one place in life that gave him much comfort and inspiration. Perhaps his stories are not as far off as some may think.

The Observatory is located at 210 Doyle Avenue on the corner of Hope Street. On the first floor, one can examine vintage equipment from the observatory's early days. The observatory is open to the public on clear Tuesday evenings. A staircase and elevator lead to a balcony, providing stargazing through several portable telescopes, including the main twelve-inch refractor.

Each year, Keith and Carl Johnson host a special tribute to the legendary writer. The event takes place at the observatory around the calendar date of his death. After the tribute, a tour to his grave and a few other Lovecraft sites round out a perfect Lovecraftian day. If you should happen to get a glimpse of the writer's ghost, then that would make it even better.

Mowry Tavern and the Clawson Curse

During the very early days of Providence, there stood an ordinary known as the Mowry Tavern. The tavern was located on the corner of Abbott and North Main Streets. It was built by Roger Mowry in 1653 and was granted license to keep a house of entertainment in 1655. His sign was set out in "ye most perspicuous place of ye saide house thereby to give notice to strangers that it is a house of entertainment."

Mowry's Tavern was the only such business in town and served as an inn, a jail, a town meetinghouse and the location for Sabbath services held by Roger Williams. Williams not only preached the word of god but also practiced his piety in other ways, for there was a young man that he took in by the name of John Clawson. Clawson was discovered in a sorry state of health and starvation by Williams, who in turn invited him into his home and offered him a position in the household as one of his servants.

The lad grew and prospered in a small but handsome way, eventually owning his own home and land while serving as the town carpenter. One winter morning, a passerby found Clawson near a clump of barberry bushes adjacent to the tavern. He had been badly bludgeoned with a broad axe about the face and chest. Some townsfolk carried him to Williams's house where, surrounded by friends and neighbors, he expired from his wounds. Before he passed, Clawson muttered the name John Hearndon, accusing him of the deed and cursing him and his future generations to be marked with split chins and be haunted by barberry bushes.

The event drew much excitement, as it was the first murder to be committed in the settlement. Despite Clawson's deathbed accusation, suspicion fell on an Indian named Waumanitt. He was apprehended and taken to the tavern for confinement until he could be tried for murder. During his confinement, the truth of Clawson's murder slowly surfaced. Waumanitt confessed it was he who sprang from the bushes and attacked Clawson with an axe as he passed by the barberry bushes.

Although the Indian confessed to the murder, there was strong belief he was paid by John Hearndon to commit the evil deed—for what specific reason is lost to antiquity. It is recorded the two were neighbors and had

The old Mowry Tavern in Providence. *From Thomas D'Agostino's private collection.*

quarreled viciously for some reason. The spot where Clawson was murdered became a dark and eerie parcel of town, and travelers were prone to pick up their pace as they passed by the barberry bushes. Horses were known to shy from the spot or kick up in protest while passing the bushes where the young man met his fate. As for the curse, generations of Hearndons were marked with unsightly split chins.

In time, the bushes that sat across from the tavern were torn down to make way for the North Burial Ground. Roger Mowry was buried there upon his death in 1666. In 1900, the decaying building was torn down to make room for a three-decker tenement house, thus ending the life of what was the oldest house in the city and host of a real haunted tale of the Blackstone Valley.

SMITHFIELD

THE "HAUNTED" CITY

In the northwest portion of Smithfield, buried deep in the woods, lies a ghost town known as Hanton City or Haunted City. The remains of this lost city sit in a wooded area also known as Island Woods due to the swampy nature of the land and the hills that rise up from the quagmire.

The abandoned town is rich with mystery as to who its founders were, why they settled there and what became of them. Many theories speculate everything from runaway slaves, British army deserters or even plague victims banished to the woods to keep them from infecting the general populace. We do know that the Hantons, an early Yankee pronunciation for Harrington, Herrindeen, Herndean or Hearndon, were numerous in the three-thousand-acre settlement. The most logical reason the people of the haunted city vanished from the area was due to the poor farming conditions and growth of industry outside the settlement. The bustling factories provided jobs and a place to live for those who migrated out of the fields and woods to join the modern world. The Hantons, however, stayed with their homesteads well into the latter half of the nineteenth century until they finally died off, leaving the area to memories and the spirits that still linger among the ruins.

Much of the remains are still visible for the curious to visit. There are numerous home foundations, wells, corncrib stilts, walls, a portion of the old school/meetinghouse and a few colonial burying grounds that seem to spring out from behind brush or appear around every corner. Hiking the

Photo of an old map showing the center of Hanton (Haunted) City. Note the ghost and jug of rum. *From Thomas D'Agostino's private collection.*

overgrown roads is quite an experience, as they are among the oldest in the state and still accessible. Although many areas of the land are private property, the Smithfield Land Trust owns a good section of Hanton City for the inquisitive to explore.

One such natural artifact of great interest is a large boulder with a basin in the center. This is known as the threshing or "thrashing" rock. Both Indians and settlers used this basin to winnow their grain, or separate the heads from the stalks. Excavations at some of the sites revealed much about the daily life of those who lived in the haunted city. Pipe fragments, ox shoes and fragments of dishes and small tools give estimates of when the place was inhabited.

The *Observer*, a local weekly publication, offered two articles in May and August 1972 about the place locals called "the Rumbly." In the articles, Hanton City is referred to as "a real village that sank into the middle of Cedar Swamp like the lost city of Atlantis."

The main road through the village was given the name Rumbly due to the rough, barely navigable condition of its surface. The paper went on to state: "There are old timers, or were until recently, who still had recollections of the 'ride through the rumbly,' that eerie, ghost-ridden place called Hanton City Road."

One of the many foundations in Hanton City. *Courtesy of Jim Ignasher.*

The "Rumbly" leading through Hanton City. *Courtesy of Jim Ignasher.*

On this road once stood a small stone building where the Hanton City folk left rum and gingerbread for those passing through to eat and drink. "They speak of a stone house by the roadside where refreshments were left for weary travelers who could pay or not, as they were able. This food, a jug of rum and some gingerbread, was supposedly set out by the mysterious Hantons."

Several old-timers hunting in the old city recalled instances where their rifles were wrenched from their hands, landing several feet away. People hiking through the old village have also heard children laughing and playing in the perimeters of the house ruins. People hiking the old roads are often overcome by a strange, fearful feeling that someone or something is watching them.

In 2015, cable television show host Charles Gardiner, along with his crew—Dan Case, Matt McDermott and David Chadronet—toured the abandoned village to see what they could find. The following incident took place at what is known as the Hermit's House. It is at this foundation where witnesses attest to have seen a misty apparition floating about near the remains of the home. At one of the foundations, Charles recorded a voice of a woman whispering. The fact that there were no women present at the time and all present were all very quiet during the EVP session made this piece of evidence quite valuable in the sphere of unexplainable activity reported within Hanton City.

A 1937 *Providence Journal* article depicted the cellar hole with a tree sprouting from it. The author estimated that the tree was about one hundred years old at that time. An 1889 article shows one of the derelict buildings still standing but in a bad state of decay. The article also related that the last of the Hantons still lived by Route 7 on the outskirts of the village.

Another area where supernatural occurences have been reported is the Brown Cemetery. The small family burying ground has about fifteen burials marked with hand-hewn fieldstones. A few of the stones are carved with crude inscriptions. One reads "A.B. 1774" and the other "D.B. May 1784."

D.B. was most likely Daniel Brown and A.B. Alice Hearnton Brown, daughter of Benjamin Hearnton. This location is another place where people have heard voices, and some spied shadows moving out of the corner of their eyes within the small cemetery. It could be paranormal or perhaps just the natural movement of the trees and brush swaying in the wind, playing tricks on them. In Hanton City, anything is possible.

There is also a site on the edge of the trail where six upright stones beckon the curious. These were most likely used for a corncrib. The home foundation with stone indents resembling shelves behind the six standing stones is in remarkable condition for its age. Hikers have also recorded EVPs at this site. In 2014, a small group of researchers encountered a voice that permeated the air, not in a loud tone but as if it was right beside the party. The voice clearly said, "inside the barn." They all froze at first, wondering where it came from, as the group was deep in the woods with no one else around. The remains of what resembled the foundation of a barn sit close to the former home.

By most accounts, Hanton City became a ghost town in the early nineteenth century, but it was not completely unoccupied until well into the twentieth century. The Daniel family lived in a house on Rocky Hill a mile into the woods from both Douglas Pike and Rocky Hill Road. The house was constantly occupied from 1936 until the 1950s, when the family finally moved out. The house had no running water or electricity. Water was drawn from a well near the home, and light was provided by the aid of kerosene lamps. After the family moved away, they continued to use it as a summer home until it was mysteriously set fire and burned in 1972. For many years, all that remained was the massive cellar, but it was filled in around 2005. When you reach the spot where the cellar hole was, a fork in the road will take you toward the best sites in the ruined village; this also includes the threshing rock and what is considered the center of the old town.

The other family to live in the Hanton City woods was the Wilcoxes. They lived there only a short time, from around 1927 until World War II. The Wilcox site is one of the first to be seen while walking up the trail from Lydia Ann Road. A 1947 map shows the home site, and it is labeled "unoccupied," which means that the buildings were still standing and probably in a habitable condition. This same map also shows the home of J.J. Daniel on the rough Rumbly of Hanton City.

There exists a few poems and stories of Hanton City to judge by even meager standards its people and what life was like there. The poems were handed down from generation to generation, retold as they heard them from their parents before:

Widow Mack and Short Ann Free
Tanner Ben and Sim Bushee

Up in Hanton City
There lived a very tall man.
He had a handsome daughter
And her name was Hittean
She was courted by Lords & Dukes,
And by many a wealthy Knight.
But no one but Philip the Darkey
Could gain her heart's delight.

The exact demise of Hanton City may never be established, but research shows that it was on its way to becoming a ghost town by the early 1800s. Some say that the old-timers of the area knew more than they would let on about what happened up there in the woods and fields of Smithfield.

There are the rumors, too, and some old people who are supposed to really
know what happened to Hanton City only answer with silence.
"So there really was a Hanton City?"
"Yup."
"And it disappeared did it?"
"Ayeh."

Although there is no hunting, there are some who still disregard the posts, so be sure to wear bright colors when traversing the trails, just in case.

More than Just Ghosts in the Mill

Note: The name and location are not divulged in respect for the property and those who are still involved with it. Please respect the privacy of this place and do not trespass, as you will be prosecuted.

Smithfield is home to several mills that are still standing and renovated for other purposes. These mills often have various businesses within their walls, including stores, offices, construction and manufacturing. Such is the case of this next story.

A friend owned a store in an old mill. I visited every Friday, as it was just around the corner from my office in the same mill. The establishment sold old records and instruments, gave music lessons and held small concerts in the main room. It was quite a popular hangout for local musicians. It also is haunted. One day, as my friend was at the register, he heard something behind him. Being the only one in the building, he thought it was just the sound of an old mill. He turned quickly and was confronted by a dark figure standing within arm's reach of him. He jumped backward with a start, and the figure quickly faded away. One afternoon I stopped by, and we chatted for a while. I picked up a vintage guitar magazine and began to flip through it. My friend was reading the daily newspaper. One of the staff walked by us toward the back rooms. Neither of us heard her open and close the entrance door but never thought anything of it. Several minutes later, she came by again, but this time we saw and heard her entering through the front door. Both confused and astounded, my friend asked her how she got back outside since there is no other way in or out than the front door. "I am just getting here now," she replied.

A close inspection of the rooms revealed no one else was in any of them. Neither of us had originally paid much heed to the figure when it passed by us in the first place. Who it was we saw slip by is still a mystery. The ghosts of the mill did not limit their roaming to the front of the building. The rear of the building housed a storage facility, some office spaces and a few more ghosts. When I rented one of the office spaces, I was often asked if anything strange had happened yet. The woman who rented the office before I occupied it was an artist. She never dared venture into the main hallway until her husband came to escort her out of the building. She often heard voices in the hall between her room and the storage lockers. Every time she went to investigate, the area was empty. The long, open hall led to a large garage door that was the only way in or out. When someone entered, the heavy door would rumble and clang on its rails, making for a very loud alarm that someone was coming or going. Each time she heard the voices, no door noise preceded or followed.

Another person had a woodworking shop in one of the larger rooms. He often took his daughter with him when he worked in the evenings. One night, she was playing with a few of the empty storage locker doors. The metal clanging was not only loud, but he also felt she should not be playing with someone else's property and scolded her for it. He then had her remain in his shop with him while he finished his work.

A few moments later, a horrible crashing sound ripped through the air, causing the man and his daughter to jump with a start. He ran out to see what the thunderous noise was. All twelve doors of the storage area had been opened at the same time. Needless to say, when the month was over, he did not renew his lease.

The ghosts may be playful or prankish on the lower floors, but the upper floor is the scariest place to be. Arlene and I decided to check out the reported ghostly activities within the old edifice. A trip to the place with friends Rich and Ally Alarie became a must. Sounds of a large building can deceive one's senses into thinking there is someone or something else wandering the long hallways. Having been a tenant there for a while, the strange sounds of the pumps, heaters, air conditioners and other apparatus that kept the old mill up to date were all too familiar to my ears.

We had just finished inspecting the first floor when we decided to try the upper floors. Nothing special transpired for some time, and then we heard it. It was the sound of heavy clomping footsteps moving across the floor above us. There was only one stairway to the third floor, and the door, as I expected, was locked. I had been given the key ahead of time just in case we dared to venture that far. We all climbed the stairs to the top floor. There was no electricity on that floor, and it was wide open, with no separate rooms. One of the businesses was offered free access for storage on that floor but had refused, asserting that something was up there and it was not nice. The framework of what was supposed to be an office sat at the far end of the room. A frame of two by fours nailed together with no partitioning walls was as far as the builder got before quitting his mission. What ever was up there was enough to scare someone out of free storage and another out of finishing their project.

With flashlights in hand, a vigil commenced. "Could you tell us who you are? Could you give us a sign of where you are so we may see you?"

At that moment, a loud crashing sound like a large chain or machine smashing into something came from behind, then from the left, then in front of us, near the far wall, then all around in rapid succession. All was quiet for a few moments before the crashing resounded two more times. When the atmosphere in the room became so heavy it was difficult to breathe, Rich left a recorder in the far corner of the room before relocating downstairs to continue investigating. Upon returning to retrieve the recorder, Rich walked into the darkness of the far corner where the device lay. Suddenly, a crashing sound like a large plank of wood bouncing off the floor broke the silence. "What did you drop, Rich?" The question was met with silence.

"Rich, did you knock something over?" Still silence.

Arlene then interjected, "Did you drop something?"

A faint voice answered, "No, something just came flying at me."

While Rich was retrieving the recorder, something threw a length of board at him. He was afraid to move or speak for fear that another would follow and hit its mark. Then came the loud crashing sounds again. Unfortunately, the video recorders did not capture any images, as whatever caused the loud bangs was not visible to the cameras.

The next day, I visited with my friend and told him what happened the night before. That is when he told me to follow him outside.

See those two new windows? I put those in. I was hired to replace all the windows on that floor. I figured after I closed the store I could go up there and replace a few every day. The first night, I brought my work light up and tools with me because there is no electricity. I got the first two windows in fast and figured this was going to be a cinch. Then this loud crashing noise started all around me. It sounded like massive chains being slammed on the floor. My light was very bright and I could see all around, but there was no one in the empty room except me and yet the noise came from all around. Those are the only two windows I put in. There was no way I was going back up there.

Come to find out, the other tenants of the building have heard the loud crashing as well. There seemed to be a lot of banging on the floor, as if whatever was up there was very angry over our intrusion. I only ventured up there one more time in the light of day. It was quiet and peaceful save for the rubble on the floor, the two old windows leaning against one of the support columns and a dozen brand-new windows still wrapped up awaiting installation.

Over time I gave up my office, as I had no more need for it. I still visit my friend on occasion, and he mentions that no one ventures up to the third floor. The place is quiet now, and the tenants like it that way—all of them.

GREENVILLE PUBLIC LIBRARY

Libraries are perfect places for haunts. It is amazing that more libraries are not home to at least one ghost. In Smithfield, the Greenville Public Library has at least one resident ghost that wanders among the many tomes.

The Jenckes family donated land to the town for a new library when the old one began to swell at its seams with the growing collection of books. Several outbuildings were razed, and the family home was moved from its old foundation to its present one on the side of the library. When the

The Greenville Public Library on Route 44/Putnam Pike. *Photo by Arlene Nicholson.*

library was built, a beautiful stone building also was donated for storage and conferences. The town eventually tore the building down to expand the parking lot. This may have set off old Mrs. Jenckes, who was a longtime trustee of the library and donator of the land in 1938. The present library was commissioned on October 18, 1955.

The library was built on the existing Jenckes house foundation and, in later years, expanded. The original basement is still part of the lower level of the library and seems to be the most haunted place in the building. Many patrons have reported the uncanny feeling of being watched by some unseen presence while on the lower floor of the library.

There is a piano in one of the rooms that has been heard playing when no one was there. Many years ago, while studying in an adjacent room in the basement, a witness suddenly heard the soft sounds of the piano, as if someone was toying with it. Upon examination and entrance into the room, the music abruptly stopped, and the room was completely empty. There was absolutely no way anyone could have left the room unseen, as the door was in full view of everyone present. These occurrences take place at random hours throughout the day and night.

Darryll Aucoin, one of the former members of the staff at the library, credited Mrs. Jenckes for the ghostly deeds. Some nights he would turn all the lights off downstairs, and by the time he was back on the first floor, they were all on again. Books would fall from the shelves in front of the staff as if an unseen hand was pulling them from their resting place.

Aucoin and another girl witnessed a whole row of books slide out of the shelf onto the floor like someone had taken their arm and pushed them from behind. The current staff occasionally hear the thud of a book fall from the shelves as if someone or something is trying to remove it from its place. Some claim it might be the spirit of the first librarian, Orra Angell. Angell was the librarian for the village in 1882, when the library was down the street across from the common. Whether it may be Mrs. Angell or Mrs. Jenkes does not make much difference, as much of the staff does not like to venture down into the lower chambers unaccompanied for fear of confronting the restless spirit.

The library is located at 573 Putnam Pike, just before Greenville Common across from William Winsor Elementary School.

THE HAUNTED SMITHFIELD TAVERN

The Resolved Waterman Tavern sits in the center of Greenville, Rhode Island, as a historic landmark and tribute to the bygone era of stagecoach travel and tavern life. The building one sees today is but a fraction of what the tavern originally looked like. The inn was originally T-shaped, with the east and western walls connected by a courtyard. This building is the earliest tavern on record in Smithfield. Resolved Waterman (1703–1746) erected the tavern in 1733 at the crossroads in Greenville just after the completion of the Providence/Putnam Turnpike. A large dining hall sat on the first floor, with a dance hall directly above. The tavern quickly became a popular stop along the busy pike; travelers and locals mingled, telling stories and the latest news over drinks and victuals, or danced the night away at hoedowns. In fact, Waterman's tavern became such a favored rest stop it rarely stayed vacant. One evening, a traveling peddler came to lodge at the inn. Unfortunately, all the rooms were full, but Mr. Waterman, being a kind man, offered him lodging in the root cellar. The traveler ate and drank his lot and share until he was ready to retire for the night. He stumbled down the narrow stairs to the makeshift accommodations to sleep off his excessive indulgence. That was the last anyone ever saw of him—in the flesh, anyway. The next morning, his bag of wares and belongings were found next to his bed, but

The restored Resolved Waterman Tavern. *Photo by Arlene Nicholson.*

he had simply vanished without a trace. It was soon agreed upon that he might have risen in the dead of night and, stumbling around in the dark, fell into the well in the basement. Resolved Waterman, fearing this and the fact that it could happen again, sealed the well and dug another in a safer, more secluded spot. Within a few weeks of this incident, guests began seeing the ghost of the peddler roaming around the building. Regulars swore it was the shade of the peddler they all shared drinks with on that fateful night he mysteriously disappeared.

Another boarder once roomed in the cellar for the evening but got the fright of his life when a pair of scissors took on wings and flew past his head. Needless to say, the guest took his belongings and cut out of the building in a hurry.

As time passed, so did the owners of the haunted inn. In 1822, the building became the home of the Smithfield Exchange Bank. The bank folded in 1856, but the massive safe stayed on the first floor of the building.

In 1936, the front section of the building was razed to allow the expansion of Putnam Pike. The last inhabitant of the house was Bessie Fish. For many years, the building stood vacant and prone to vandals. In 2003, the Smithfield Preservation Society acquired the crumbling building and began renovations. The building is now a museum, complete with an upper meeting hall, the safe on the first floor where banking was done and other important historical artifacts throughout the building.

The ghost of the peddler is still said to haunt the structure as you read this. The home is occasionally open for tours, and those who venture into the building get a glimpse into history. Who knows? You may even get a tour from a man resembling an eighteenth-century peddler.

UPTON

UPTON'S STONE CHAMBER

According to archaeo-astronomers James Mavor and Byron Dix, New England's stone chambers follow a certain line starting at the Upton Chamber and culminating in Thompson, Connecticut, where another such beehive chamber exists. Some scholars claim that these may have been made by the praying Indians Reverend John Eliot converted during the seventeenth century, while others have found evidence suggesting they may have been here long before Eliot's quest.

The stone chamber in Upton comprises an entrance tunnel 14.3 feet long, about 4.5 feet tall and 2.8 to 3.3 feet wide. This tunnel leads to a beehive-shaped room 11.0 feet in diameter by 10.5 feet at the top of the roof. The stonework is corbelled, meaning the stones were placed on top of one another in an offset manner, creating what looks like a beehive. The roof is topped with a large capstone and is covered by earth. Archaeologist Malcolm Pearson once owned the chamber. In fact, it was that very stone structure that interested him as a child enough to want to enter the field of archaeology. William Goodwin, an amateur archaeologist, known for his work at Mystery Hill in North Salem, New Hampshire, featured the structure in his book *The Ruins of Great Ireland in New England*.

In the text, Goodwin included photographs by Pearson and architectural drawings by Professor V.F. Fagan. It was proposed that an ancient Irish

Entrance to the Upton Chamber. *Photo by Arlene Nicholson.*

culture built the chamber, as such chambers are found in Ireland and other European tombs dating back five thousand years. It is one of two beehive-style chambers in New England, the other being in East Thompson, Connecticut.

The actual age of the chamber is unknown. The structure was in existence when the first settlers arrived in the area around 1734. The local Indians noted that it had always been there. Its use remained an enigma until James W. Mavor and Byron Dix began investigating the chamber and its position in regard to the heavens. The two hypothesized that the chamber was constructed and used around AD 700 to 750 to observe the setting of Pleiades, the summer solstice around AD 670 and the other stars of importance in the telling of the seasons. By careful examination and surveying, mostly by sight, they located stone mounds on nearby Pratt Hill. The direct lines from the opening of the chamber to these mounds were conclusive; the chamber may have been used as an astronomical calendar, but by whom is still a mystery.

The best guess so far is Celtic people who were known to have visited the region long before England or other exploring countries. There are other such chambers and carvings in boulders, structures and astronomical

Inside the Upton Chamber looking toward the entrance. *Photo by Arlene Nicholson.*

calendars around New England that tell of an ancient race but offer very little as to their exact identity.

The Upton Stone Chamber can be seen in Heritage Park in Upton, located at 18 Elm Street. When you pull into the small parking area facing the fence, look in your rearview mirror for the stone bench by a tree near a small shed. Walk past that tree, and you will see the entrance to the chamber. It is that easy—a lot easier than figuring out who the original builders were. I guess the answer lies in the past, told only in tales of long ago.

UXBRIDGE

THE CROWN AND EAGLE MILL

Blackstone Valley may be the birthplace of industry, but it also reigns as a region rich with scenery, history, adventure and a haven for some of the most prolific haunts in all New England. One such place is the small town of Uxbridge, Massachusetts, where in some cases, time and progress are at a standstill, but the ghosts are not.

Uxbridge was incorporated on June 27, 1727. Like other rural New England settlements, it was mostly agricultural, but the bountiful waters of the Blackstone River would soon change the farming community into a bustling manufacturing village. Large mills began to pop up along the river, making Uxbridge a manufacturing hub between the cities of Providence, Rhode Island, and Worcester, Massachusetts.

One mill of significant importance was the Crown and Eagle. The first incarnation of the complex was the Clapp Mill at 84 East Hartford Avenue, built by Forbes and Benjamin Clapp in 1810. The mill manufactured thread—the first mill to do so in the valley. Robert Rogerson had bigger ideas for the structure. He purchased the mill around 1823 and turned it into housing. He then built two new mills, the Crown (1823–25) and the Eagle (1827) over the Mumford River, a tributary of the Blackstone River.

The new complex was in keeping with the mill village idea or Rhode Island System of the time, consisting of housing, a store, a community building and the two mills. One noted feature of both mills was the clerestory monitor roofs—the first of their kind in Massachusetts. Such a roof admitted light through long windows at the top of the building to bring in natural daylight for better illumination within the mill. The famous Whitin family of nearby Northbridge purchased the mill in 1841 and renamed it the Uxbridge Cotton Mill. The factory stayed in business until the early 1920s, when it finally closed its doors. For a half a century, the only occupants of the crumbling structure were the ghosts of those who once toiled in the mill, either left behind by some tragic moment or just remnants of a time when the mill whirred with life.

In those subsequent years, neighbors of the abandoned building were subjected to strange ghostly phenomena that took place within the mill. Often they would see faces peering out of the windows of the otherwise derelict edifice. The woeful faces seemed to peer out through the broken panes as if looking for eternal peace. Witnesses attested that the visages were "fuzzy," as if slightly out of focus. If close enough to the windows, one may see right through the ghostly features, sending a shiver down the spine at the sight of such an unearthly countenance.

The locals knew well to shun the edifice because of the uneasy feeling the structure gave to all who passed by it. Corroborating reports circulated of ghosts in early twentieth-century work attire emerging from the factory as if they were reliving the end of their workday. Many whose fathers or grandfathers worked the looms and spindles in the mill were well aware that the ghosts never left even after the doors were boarded up for the last time. Most of them were housed in the building provided for them by the mill owners, so it would seem likely that they would linger, as the mill complex was the only existence they knew.

Tragedy struck in 1975 when the mill burned down, but the fire did not end the sightings of the phantom workers that lingered in and around the mill. On various occasions, witnesses saw figures moving within the ruins. Assuming it to be curious folk wandering within the burned out structure, they approached the people to warn of the dangerous remains they were investigating. The do-gooder would get the fright of their life when the person they were trying to warn would vanish in front of them. The ghosts within the mill are just one haunt. There seems to be much more to the haunting than just the spirits that still roam within its confines. At one time, the mill itself was the source of the phantom phenomenon. Several witnesses claimed to have actually seen the mill intact as if the fire never destroyed the enormous structure. A few daring residents reported that on those strange occasions, they approached the deserted mill and hastily left after being overcome with an unexplainable fright. When they looked back at the mill, to their horror, they saw the burned shell of what was once the factory.

People also reported having seen the mill consumed in flames and the frightened face of a child in one of the windows. In an instant, the vision would be gone, and in its place would be the silent and gutted remains of what was once the Crown and Eagle of Uxbridge. If these reports have any validity, then it would be safe to conclude that the land the complex was built on possesses some sort of energy to manifest such apparitions. The accounts of the ghost mill are numerous and varied. Whether they are all true or not is a matter of conjecture.

The mill was rebuilt in the early 1990s by investors as a housing project for the elderly. The original remains of the mill can be easily recognized in contrast to the more modern wall structure that was erected on top of the stonework that was once the great and haunted Crown and Eagle Mills. The residents have nothing dramatic to report since the rebirth of the building. Perhaps the ghosts of the Crown and Eagle have finally retired into that great eternal sleep.

THE UXBRIDGE TAFT WHO BOUGHT A HAUNTED MILL

Everyone in Uxbridge and surrounding towns know of the famous Taft family. Their roots go back to the first settlers of the land, and many a prominent Taft has risen to fame, including the twenty-seventh president of the United States, William Howard Taft, whose parents hailed from New England. The Taft family was instrumental in the manufacturing business and is credited for several mills in the region. One Taft, Orsmus, purchased a haunted mill in Foster, Rhode Island.

Orsmus was born on January 1, 1795, in Uxbridge. He began to work in mills at an early age and saved his money, buying shares in the companies while working his way up the corporate ladder. On October 29, 1821, he married Margaret Smith, and together they had eleven children. Their first child, Royal Chapin Taft, would later become the thirty-ninth governor of Rhode Island.

In 1837, Orsmus sold his shares to the factory in Uxbridge and decided to branch out. On June 6, 1844, he bought three undivided shares to the Foster Woolen Manufactory from Orra Potter, widow of factory

The only known photograph of the Ramtail Factory taken about the time Orsmus Taft owned the establishment. *From Thomas D'Agostino's private collection.*

co-founder Olney E. Potter. Several family members, including a son-in-law, Peleg Walker, founded the Foster Woolen Manufactory and the small village that surrounded the mill in 1813. In 1817, Jonathan Bucklin committed suicide in the factory after losing his land to factory owners William and Olney E. Potter. The Potters agreed to loan him money using his land as collateral. When he failed to repay the loan, the land was auctioned off to repay the note.

Tragedy struck once more in 1822 when co-owner Peleg Walker was found dead in the factory from an apparent suicide. There is speculation by way of certain deeds and land conveyance that he may have met with foul play. Either way, shortly after his death, his ghost began ringing the bell to the mill in the dead of night. The rest of the owners soon removed the bell, but Peleg had more in store for them. Several nights later, the workers in the mill houses were thrown from their sleep at the chime of midnight by the mill running full tilt. The following night, the wheel began turning again at the witching hour—only this time, moving opposite the flow of the river.

People began to vacate the homes for fear of the ghost, but that did not stop Peleg from making his rounds. Those traveling by the mill at night often saw the glowing of a candle lantern roaming among the buildings as Mr. Walker made his nightly rounds. His ghost was spied several times entering and leaving the buildings he so loved in life. By the time Taft bought the shares, the factory was well known for its ghosts, and few dared to step foot inside at any wage.

The disturbing incidents did not deter Mr. Taft from his goal in securing the ownership of the small mill, for by August 1844, he had convinced the other widow, Catherine Potter, to sell her shares in the establishment, thus retaining full ownership of the little mill and village. It is not known if Orsmus was aware at that time the mill was haunted, but it can be assured he would soon find out.

By 1844, there had been two suicides and one sudden death associated with the mill. Bucklin in 1817, Walker in 1822 and Olney E. Potter (who some maintain may have had something to do with the untimely demise of Peleg Walker) in 1831, exactly nine years to the day Peleg Walker died.

The factory and village had taken on a curse that remained throughout its existence. By day, machines would turn on and off by themselves, and items would disappear and reappear in other places. By night, the ghostly lantern could be spied roaming the mill grounds, moving from building to building. There would be no success for subsequent owners, and Orsmus was no exception. By 1847, he had taken out a second mortgage on the mill and was forced to sell it for what he could. Welcome Arnold purchased the mill, and from there it changed hands several more times before burning in 1873.

Orsmus Taft died on July 8, 1880, and is now buried in the Prospect Hill Cemetery with his wife and other family members. The remains of the mill and village still tenant ghosts of long past eras. Two other deaths associated with the mill have strengthened the ghostly happenings at Ramtail. Richard Salisbury was said to take refuge in one of the decrepit homes when he saw fit to have his fill of drink. The solace afforded him his privacy to enjoy his chosen libation without interruption. It was in one of the rundown shacks that he passed away, and his ghost is also said to roam the area. Betsy Grayson, a squatter at one of the Ramtail homes, drowned when she attempted to draw water from the Ponaganset River. The swift current pulled her and her wooden bucket into the water, where she apparently banged her head on one of the many boulders in the stream. This was December 20, 1860, several years after Orsmus Taft relinquished the keys to the factory. It is probably a fortunate move on his part, as had he kept the cursed factory, it can only be speculated what fate he might have suffered.

WOONSOCKET

PRECIOUS BLOOD CEMETERY

Blackstone, Massachusetts, was named in honor of the first European settler to the area, Reverend William Blackstone. There are plenty of haunts that befall this historic hamlet. Precious Blood Cemetery, located at the intersection of Diamond Hill Road and Rathbun Street, is one place that truly deserves mention as one of the eeriest places to visit. The cemetery is located in both, Woonsocket, Rhode Island, and Blackstone. Upon entering the main entrance on the Rhode Island side, the cemetery looks ornate and magnificent, but the bulk of the graveyard that rests in Blackstone takes on a more ominous tone. Various paranormal groups have visited this burial ground due to the massive amount of paranormal activity within the confines of the necropolis.

Even during the brightest of days, the hue of the burial ground takes on a dark, overcast shade. The grounds were officially closed to any new plots as of May 31, 1955, but people still inter their loved ones in the earth of Precious Blood. Makeshift wooden crosses made from two-by-fours, logs and even fence railings with handwritten names and epitaphs adorn the landscape amid the marble and granite markers. Other strange sights await the curious in this peculiar place of eternal repose.

Investigators photographed orbs floating over gravestones, and visitors have witnessed shadowy figures flitting about the tombs. Residents around

Precious Blood Cemetery in Woonsocket and Blackstone. *Photo by Arlene Nicholson.*

the cemetery attest to the specters that still roam the grounds for one reason or another. Some investigators claim to have recorded the voices of those buried among the silent and long resting in the graveyard. Interred in the cemetery is Marie Rose Ferron, the only known case of stigmata in New England history. Stigmata are the appearance of marks on the body resembling those of Christ at the time he was crucified. The marks strangely appear and disappear without explanation or warning.

Marie Rose was born in Quebec, Canada, in 1902, but the family eventually migrated to Woonsocket. She was the tenth child of a very religious family. Each child was to represent the rosary. Coincidentally, the tenth rosary is crucifixion. Although Marie Rose was born with a rare, crippling form of arthritis, the infliction did not seem to take away her spirit for helping others. She was known to have incredible healing powers, sharing them with all who came to the parish for salvation and help. Her followers later petitioned her for sainthood, but the Vatican refused to grant it.

Marie Rose Ferron died in 1936 at the age of thirty-three, the same age of Christ when he was crucified. Little Rose, as she was and still is called, foretold her own death and died of natural causes brought about by her infliction. She was buried in Precious Blood Cemetery. Her grave is about two hundred feet up the right-hand road at the first intersection. After her death, she was exhumed for further proof of stigmata. It was conclusive. She was reburied and now seems to heal from the grave to this very day. Scores of religious pilgrims from all over the world flock to her simple stone to absorb the healing energy said to radiate from her burial plot.

Investigators allege to hear her voice speaking to them when they are near the gravesite.

The grave of Marie Rose Ferron, New England's only known Stigmatee. *Photo by Arlene Nicholson.*

Another reason why there is so much activity at Precious Blood might be due to the catastrophe that fell upon it during the flood of August 1955. First, there was Hurricane Connie. Although just a tropical storm by the time it hit the region, it still dropped nine inches of water on the city of Woonsocket and other areas between August 13 and 14, 1955. One week later Hurricane Diane swept through, bringing more rain to the already tasked rivers and ponds. The heavy rains broke open the horseshoe dam of Harris Pond. Houses and businesses were swept away by the raging waters of the mighty Blackstone River. The pond spilled out into the city, taking a corner of the cemetery away with it. It was reported the rushing wave of water reached up to twenty feet in height by the time it hit the retaining wall of the cemetery.

More than fifty caskets were splintered, dispersing their remains into the floodwaters. Some floated out into the middle of the streets, while others were washed out to sea never to be found again. Pieces of caskets and remains dotted the areas of Social Street and the adjoining roads. Backyards became gathering points for the unearthed remains of the deceased. A few made their way down the river and ended up in places such as Slater Mill in Pawtucket.

A view of the back half of Precious Blood Cemetery. *Photo by Arlene Nicholson.*

After the flood, many of the disinterred were recovered and brought to the mausoleum at Precious Blood. They were later transported to St. Jeans, where new headstones were put in place and the deceased reburied. Some needed new coffins while others, still in their sarcophaguses, were recovered from the river as well as the bottom of the ocean floor. Some were reported reburied with the wrong stones marking their graves.

It was a gruesome task that many believe left an indelible mark on the atmosphere of the cemetery. The orbs, voices and spirits roaming among the sixteen thousand graves could be the ghosts of those who were lost or lost their loved ones they were buried next to when the flood of 1955 dragged them away.

There is one amazing story about the tragedy that is still told to this day. A husband and wife lived across from the cemetery. While the wife was very ill and in her last days, she swore to her husband that she would return if he married before the period of mourning passed.

When she passed away, she was buried in Precious Blood Cemetery, and her husband, against her wishes, quickly remarried. The hurricanes arrived soon after, and her casket was one of the many that washed down Social Street. In a weird twist of events, the casket came to rest across the street from his home. The widower looked out his door and saw her nameplate on the half-open lid with her hair and arm sticking out. He immediately suffered a heart attack and died. They are now both buried at the cemetery, where she can forever keep an eye on him.

WORCESTER

WORCESTER COMMON

Imagine having a splendid picnic on the grass of the town common. Daily life is rolling by, and the natural wildlife stays busy with their affairs. Suddenly, a hand juts up from the earth, followed by another. Within moments, rotting corpses are emerging from the ground all around. Sounds like a scene from a zombie apocalypse movie, but if it were to be, the best candidate for that location would be the Worcester Common.

The Worcester Common originally was part of a burial ground established in 1730. Between that date and 1795, it was the only burial ground being used by the town. Town records state, "Ye selectmen do-as soon as may-state out a burying place and measure ye out the lines thereof."

The earliest recorded death found in the cemetery was that of Hannah Hubbard, wife of John Hubbard, who died on April 18, 1727, at age twenty-seven. The total number of burials varies, having reached about four hundred interments before a new burying ground, the Hope Cemetery, was established. In 1789, the town council voted that "Officers of the Artillery have liberty of erecting a gun house where the old stable now stands at the west end of the burying ground leaving 12 feet between the gate leading into said burying ground and said gun house."

The Hope Cemetery was a garden cemetery—the new rage of the time—and the common burial ground became sorely neglected. Burials in

Worcester Common, built over a burying ground. The present stones are imitations placed outward for easy reading. *Photo by Arlene Nicholson.*

the common burying yard ceased around 1824. In 1846, William S. Barton took the painstaking effort to record all the epitaphs on the tombstones in the common. The book was published in limited quantities two years later. It was almost a prophetic gesture for, in 1853, the town council voted to lay the stones over their respected graves and then cover the whole common with several feet of soil. Family members were given the opportunity to remove the stones and even the remains. Some stones were taken by family and friends and later came into the possession of the Worcester Historical Society. *Massachusetts Guide to Places and People* includes the burial ground in its walking tour of Worcester: "A Hidden Graveyard lies in the area between Salem Square and the Bigelow shaft. In it are the graves of several hundred citizens buried between 1730 and 1795. In 1854 the headstones were recorded, laid flat on the graves, and the whole area covered with earth and seeded."

For years, the Old Norwich and Worcester Railroad had tracks that ran across the common until the first Union Station opened in 1875. At that point, the tracks across the common were no longer needed and were removed.

In 1968, during construction, 111 remains were removed and reburied in the Hope Cemetery. Of those that were exhumed, only 47 were identified and relocated along with their markers. The other 64 were buried with a memorial to commemorate the reinterment of their remains.

All traces of the burial ground have long disappeared, and as you read this, the remains of about three hundred early residents of the city still lie in repose under the dirt of the common. The small fenced-in lot that marks the site is filled with reproductions of some of the original stones. One telltale sign that the stones are only props is that they all face each section of fence so the viewers may read them from the other side. The original burials would have all faced the same direction, as it was custom to bury the deceased facing east so they might rise to greet their lord in his second coming.

Next time you visit the Worcester Common, remember that you are actually in an old burying ground. Even if you do not see the graves, they are still there below, silently resting and waiting for the second coming.

WORCESTER'S HOPE CEMETERY

Worcester's Hope Cemetery is a hodgepodge of sights and scenery. Established in 1854, it became Worcester's sixth cemetery, and many of the graves from other burial grounds around the city that came before were reinterred there. There is a section where cannons are on display as a war memorial. A firemen's memorial area and a section where children are buried also grace the landscape. Many renowned people also lay in repose there like Robert Goddard, the father of modern rocketry; famous gun and bicycle maker Iver Johnson; poet Elizabeth Bishop; and several noted politicians and war heroes.

The cemetery has over twenty thousand interments, the oldest dating before 1750. There is one area that seems to get the most attention from paranormal investigators. In one area of the cemetery stands a tall grave marker with an angel holding Jesus in its arms. It is here that people have not only heard the ominous laughter of children, but they also claim to have witnessed the ghost of a little girl praying in front of the monument. One person reported to have seen the little girl walking on the lane near the aforementioned grave. She and her friend thought nothing of it, however; as they walked back the same way, the figure was still there. When they approached the little girl, she ran between a few tombstones but never came out from the other side of them. She mysteriously vanished before emerging from the other side of the stones.

Another woman visiting a family member's grave saw the same girl praying. She smiled at the girl, and the little girl smiled back before fading away right in front of her.

Others have heard the laughter of children around them as they passed by the children's graves. Some have witnessed a tall woman tending flowers near some of the newer graves. She is spotted in the summer and, when approached, vanishes before she can be confronted.

Iver and Mary Johnson's daughter Nettie died in 1874 at the age of five. Perhaps her voice is one of the otherworldly sounds that emanate from beyond the grave. Visitors to the cemetery often hear ghostly footsteps following them although no one is visible to create them. Voices of final sermons break the tranquil stillness, yet no funeral service can be seen among the tombstones that grace the scenery. Garden cemeteries originally were places for families to gather and visit their loved ones, picnic and stroll about the grounds. At the Hope Cemetery, it seems the interred still follow that trend as well.

THE WORCESTER CATACOMBS

In 1930, several articles were published in the *Worcester Telegram* after a man accidentally discovered an underground passageway leading to about thirty rooms roughly forty feet below the city of Worcester. The tunnels and chambers were made of brick, with sturdy columns supporting them. It was later found that at least three entrances were known to exist in the basements of various businesses. The tunnels had been long neglected and faded into history, as no one had any idea who created them or for what purpose. They were once again forgotten until a man named Charles Longeway Sr. discovered the old articles while researching a project. This began his lifelong journey into the origin of the underground catacombs.

Longeway later worked as a draftsman for the City of Worcester and as a civil engineer for the State of Massachusetts. His research led to many theories and stories regarding the labyrinth of rooms. He recently published a book, *Worcester's Forgotten Catacombs*, chronicling his research and discoveries.

One theory put forth is that they were built for the Underground Railroad—another was for gambling and drinking. One proposal claimed they were used as an old jail. One more possibility asserted they were cellars to buildings that were raised when portions of the city were graded, leaving

Entrance to a section of the Worcester underground tunnels. *Photo by Arlene Nicholson.*

the rooms deep below the surface. Whatever the reason, the actual truth has eluded Longeway and many others. One thing is almost certain; they were built in the eighteenth century or the early nineteenth century.

Stories abound about how the tunnels were used by officials in the early days of the twentieth century to sneak from their offices to the drinking establishments that were connected via the basements. One Webster woman recalled her mother telling her of the catacombs. Her mother worked in the display department at Denholm and McKay on Main Street from the mid-1960s until the early 1970s. The store was among the buildings that sat above one of the tunnels. She frequently mentioned descending into the catacombs to retrieve items that she and her co-workers utilized in decorating the store. Another person related how he and his friends would sneak down into the tunnels to party back in the 1960s while attending college in Worcester. Although they were known to a handful of people, they remained mostly mysterious to the general public until Longeway's recent research once again brought their existence to light.

Longeway, in his attempts to flesh out the truth behind these rooms, decided to try a more esoteric approach. He figured if history could not provide answers, maybe the ghosts of the tunnels might. It was a long shot, but there really was nowhere else to turn at that point. A group was put together, consisting of Longeway, a few close family members and friends, Arlene and me and two reporters called in to record and write about the event.

On a Sunday morning, armed with paranormal investigative equipment, the group entered a section of the catacombs through the cellar of a building. The walls are English brick two layers thick, with the bricks running at a ninety-degree angle after every seven layers. The limestone mortar is old and dry, but the structural architecture was obviously still sturdy and well designed to withstand the centuries. The windows and doors are arched at the top with the same style brick. One window was sealed with a more modern brick.

Most of the entrances have been walled up for one reason or another and may not be traceable. Nonetheless, there are a few places where some accessibility, though limited, can be gained. The group proceeded to perform its mission, asking questions brought about by the use of tarot cards, an effective and successful method we have adopted over the years.

Dowsing rods were employed to feel out any energy. The rods spun about freely when questions were asked. Of course, being close to water sources could have created some mixed results, but either way, the rods were moving, thus proving they were legitimate tools for divination. With recorders and cameras running, questions about the history of the catacombs were posed. Who built them? Why were they built? What year is it? The cards gave other great clues for questions, such as who financed the construction of the underground system and how long were the tunnels in use?

There is a well-documented account of a fight that took place in the center room, a 130- by 18-foot apartment in 1850, with English fighting star Gem Mace and another opponent whose name has been lost to antiquity.

There are several comprehensive books on the history of Worcester and Worcester County, yet none make any mention of the underground tunnels and catacombs. The EVPs recorded, though not conclusive, did provide some possible answers to the history and purpose of the catacombs. During the EVP session, everyone was so quiet, you could hear a pin drop. When the recordings were reviewed, several strange answers were captured on the recorder. One question was as to why the system was built. A whispery, gruff-voiced answer was heard saying "Fun. Smoke."

One of the brick walls in the underground tunnels. *Photo by Arlene Nicholson.*

Another query was what year it was, and a soft voice slowly answered, "1925."

Other EVPs recorded were "so cold," "thank you" and one that was indistinguishable when asked who built the rooms.

Another peculiar spot in the general area aboveground where the catacombs lie was a long, rectangular dirt section in a parking lot. The parking attendant divulged that it was some sort of a staircase leading to tunnels that had been sealed, and the pavement over it never quite stayed intact. There are stories the old-timers told of the catacombs and people who used them to travel from one building to another, but the purpose of their construction and age still remains a mystery. All we have to go by at this point is what research uncovered and the recordings of the voices from beyond.

The Palladium

The Worcester Palladium, also known as the Palladium or Palladium Theatre, located at 261 Main Street, opened its doors in 1928 as the Plymouth Theatre. In 1980, it was renamed E.M. Loews Center for the Performing Arts before

The Palladium is a great venue for music and home to a few ghosts. *Photo by Arlene Nicholson.*

receiving its present moniker. The main room has a seating capacity of 2,160, while a smaller upstairs room holds 500 people. Major acts go as far back as the Three Stooges to present-day metal bands. In fact, the Palladium has been home to the New England Metal and Hardcore Festival for sixteen years and hosted the Rock and Shock Festival for the past eleven years.

When the theater is not filled with the sounds of music, another noise reverberates through its chambers. Disembodied footsteps are heard moving about the building in areas where no human is present, and a glowing ball of light is occasionally seen floating above the balcony of the main room. There is a report dating back several decades of corpses discovered in one of the dressing rooms. I have yet to uncover a newspaper article to substantiate this, even though it does make for a macabre scene that would perpetuate a haunt. Other people claim to have seen ghostly figures roaming about the foyer and stairs. During a photo shoot for a band, the members kept saying that they felt like they were in *The Shining* while shooting in the upstairs office area.

There are also stories circulating of children who died during the shows many years ago by stunts and props gone awry. A man fell through the skylight to his death. A general manager got hit in the head by a vase that flew across the room, and a maintenance worker had a door suddenly close on his hand. A person tried to communicate with the ghosts of the Palladium by holding an EVP session. When he played the recorder back, a voice rang through, saying, "Get out!" That is exactly what he did.

In the early days of the city, some immigrants were killed on the property where the building now sits. Could the report of corpses in a dressing room have been none other than the visages of these unfortunates reappearing on the spot they met their untimely demise? There are also rumors that an Indian burial ground may have been displaced to accommodate the structure. The building was known to have a small entry leading to the mysterious underground catacombs of Worcester. In the parking lot between the theater and the Dead Horse Hill Restaurant is a large rectangular area that has been filled in with stonework and sand. Asphalt will not adhere to the spot, so it is quite visible. This appears to be one of the original entrances into the catacombs, which run under both buildings.

JOHN W. HIGGINS ARMORY

Alas, the famous museum at 100 Barber Avenue is no longer, but its legacy lives on in both memory and memorabilia, as much of the museum's two thousand–plus pieces are now housed at the Worcester Art Museum at 55 Salisbury Street in Worcester. Although the pieces vacated the building after the museum closed at the end of its eighty-two-year run in 2013, it is doubtful that all the spirits that lingered in the old museum went with them.

The museum was constructed in 1930 by John Woodman Higgins (born September 1, 1874) to house his extensive and eclectic collection of arms and armor. It opened in 1931 as the largest collection of its kind in the western hemisphere. It was then known as "The Museum of Steel and Armor." The four-story art deco building sat next to Higgins's pressed steel factory and was designed by Boston architect Joseph D. Leland. *Massachusetts Guide to Places and People* tells of the armory as such:

> *The John Woodman Higgins Armory (open weekdays 7-6), maintained by the Worcester Pressed Steel Co., is designed after the castle of Prince Eugene Hohenwefen at Salzburg, Austria. To the right is the Medieval Wing, where silent rows of armor-clad figures stand surrounded by their banners and arms, while at the far end of the hall three mounted knights are poised in medieval pageantry. Behind the mounted figures hangs a Gobelin tapestry that once adorned the palace of Louis XIV.*

By the time the museum closed, it was the second-largest arms and armor collection in the country, falling just behind the Metropolitan Museum of Art in New York City.

Higgins died on October 19, 1961, at the age of eighty-seven years, but that did not stop him from caring for his prized possessions. Employees and guests of the museum often reported seeing Higgins roaming the halls long after his mortal frame was laid to rest. This would be quite reasonable, as he

Inside the old Higgins Armory. *Photo by Arlene Nicholson.*

Armor stands guard at the old Higgins Armory. *Photo by Arlene Nicholson.*

poured his whole life, heart and soul into collecting and learning about the artifacts that he so proudly displayed. The other haunts are not so easy to peg down to any particular person.

Black shadows were often spied moving through the vast exhibit rooms, and mysterious footsteps could be heard echoing through the chambers. Some claimed they sounded almost metallic, like shoes of armor clanking on the floor. Music would occasionally reverberate through the building along with the clanging of metal as if someone was in the throes of some otherworldly swordplay. Guests complained of being touched by someone only to turn around and find they were quite alone within the perimeter they occupied.

It would be safe to say with such pieces of history there must have been more than a few spirits that clung to their ancient attire. Some, without doubt, were the death suits of those who once donned them. Perhaps their spirit still resides within them, waiting for that final heroic act in battle.

By the Way

Waterfront Mary's

Waterfront Mary's on Birch Island Road in Webster, Massachusetts, has been a regular stop for many residents over the years. Webster abuts the towns of the Blackstone Valley, and the restaurant is located on Lake Chargoggagoggmanchauggagoggchaubunagungamaugg (yes, it is the longest place name in the United States), or Webster Lake for short. Mary Dow started the establishment and ran it for four decades. Mary and her longtime companion, Charles Russell (Magoo) McGeary, still linger in her former business years after their mortal tenure on this earth has ended.

On December 29, 2003, the *Boston Globe* ran a small story in the obituaries on Mary and her partner. Mary Dow, an Ohio native, started her career in the 1940s as a waitress in Florida and Las Vegas. She claimed to have served Elvis Presley dinner while working at a restaurant in Las Vegas. Mary had her own flamboyant sense of style that set her apart from anyone else. Always seen in Hawaiian outfits or sarongs, and a large, flashy hat, she was easily distinguished in a crowd.

With Mary and Magoo at the helm, Waterfront Mary's became the Cheers of Webster, where everyone knew one another, what they drank and how they were feeling at the time. It still boasts that friendly accommodating atmosphere today.

Her bold style of dress matched her personality. She was often known to eject unruly patrons or decide it was time to shut the place down for the night if things got a bit out of hand. Everyone listened to her and respected her. Some of the ousted customers often begged to come back and were given a probation period. Those who remember her certainly loved her.

McGeary was a lifelong resident of Webster, earning a Purple Heart and two Bronze Stars during World War II. He was known as the witty Irishman who co-managed the establishment and was admired by everyone. According to the obituaries, Mary died on December 23, 2003, at the age of eighty-four. Charles had passed a few days earlier on December 17, at the age of eighty-one.

Tracy Lis purchased the restaurant at an estate sale in 2004 and has owned Waterfront Mary's since. Tracy has kept the spirit of Mary alive in the décor of the restaurant, but Tracy believes Mary's spirit never really left. Tracy, her staff and many others have experienced firsthand that Mary is still tending to her business.

Laura Gleim is a bartender with several years of tenure at Waterfront Mary's. Gleim is no stranger to the spirits of the club:

Waterfront Mary's is a local legend for spirits of all kinds. *Photo by Arlene Nicholson.*

One night we had a small event where only the upstairs was open. After we closed the whole place, I shut the lights off and closed the door to the upstairs room. As we were leaving, Tracy asked, "I thought you turned off all the lights?" I turned around, and all the upstairs lights were on. We both left the building in a hurry. I got into my van while leaving the parking lot and turning my van in the direction of the door: all the lights turned off.

Tracy further agreed with Laura:

This is not the only time the spirits of the building have decided to light up the place. I've received numerous calls from the neighbors in the middle of the night telling me that Waterfront Mary's was lit up like a Christmas tree.

Other staff members have left in haste after lights would inexplicably turn on randomly in the building. When asked if any lights were on a timer, Tracy stated they have no timers for anything at all in the building. Everything is done manually, from the lights to the coolers to the alarms.

The second-floor taproom boasts a massive brass and marble bar with etched mirrors and ebony posts that was featured at the 1893 Chicago World's Fair. Perhaps the beautiful bar came with a few spirits of the other kind. No one is sure at present, as there is not much history available on the restaurant to glean. An incident took place at the bar one afternoon with Laura and a few customers who knew Mary. Laura reported:

There was a time two years ago when we had the upstairs open for dinner. A few people were standing at the bar, and they were talking about Mary and how she disliked remotes. I was the only one behind the bar, and the remote was about ten feet away from me, and no one was near it. As they were talking about Mary, the remote suddenly flew to the floor.

Footsteps are often heard in the upstairs bar and lounge. One employee, while tending the place alone, went upstairs to get something. Tracy's father, Wayne, is often there, so she assumed he was walking around upstairs when she heard footsteps. She called out to Wayne and, when she heard no answer, searched the upstairs for him, but there was no one else in the place beside herself. She quickly left the building.

A former employee, while working alone in the building, heard the sound of ballroom music and people dancing upstairs, reminiscent of the days when Mary was the owner.

Based on the accounts provided by Tracy and Laura, coupled with the research we found on Mary, we arranged a visit to investigate the restaurant before it was to open for the season. Following are some of the incidents that transpired during the visit:

The jukebox mysteriously sprang to life, playing a song that we would later find out was called "Hallelujah," Tracy and Laura's favorite. The song played until the end, and all was quiet again.

While recording an EVP session, a bright orb was seen and disappeared "into" the bar. When we asked, "Mary, is that you with us?" within seconds, a loud bang emanated from the last bench in the upstairs taproom.

One of the closet doors unlatched and slowly swung open; at the same time, the men's room light also turned on.

Low voices between a man and a woman (slightly drowned out by the hum of the coolers) become audible to us.

There were two clopping sounds, like someone walking down the two small stairs from the hallway to the bar. A close friend of Mary and Magoo re-created the exact sound heard on the recorder. She explained that Magoo, who sustained an injury in the military, would grab the side of the doorway while entering the bar and clop down the two stairs leading behind the bar.

The upstairs bench at Waterfront Mary's that was kicked during a vigil. *Photo by Arlene Nicholson.*

The door with the two stairs leading behind the bar where the EVP of "Magoo" was recorded entering. *Photo by Arlene Nicholson.*

It is always an exciting evening with the spirits of Waterfront Mary's. Based on the evidence and testimonies of those who knew Mary and Magoo, the couple still likes to hang out in the restaurant affectionately known as the Cheers of Webster, Massachusetts.

GRANVILLE'S PUB

The town of Spencer lies on the outer boundary of the Blackstone Valley. Although not technically part of the region, it is still rich with history in regard to being a once thriving mill village. The mills may be long gone, but the old-timers still recount tales of how their parents and grandparents toiled in the long-gone edifices.

Many would leave the mills after a long day at work and pay a visit to one of the various local bars that dotted the small streets along the center of town. One in particular is now called Granville's Pub, located at 40 Chestnut Street in a neighborhood of factory homes and other small businesses. Owners Vance Granville and Jeanne Robertson have kept the bar since

Granville's Pub is one of the last of its kind in town, and it is haunted. *Photo by Arlene Nicholson.*

1999, but the building goes back to 1890. In fact, Vance's father used to visit the pub, as did Vance when he became of legal age to frequent such an establishment. Jeanne had this to say: "There were six pubs right in this little stretch. Only two are left, but at one time all the locals and factory workers would fill these places. It was and still is a very friendly atmosphere."

So friendly that some, including the first owners of Granville's, still like to make an appearance now and then.

Shortly after purchasing the business, Jeanne and Vance had their first encounter with the spirits of 40 Chestnut Street. Vance related the whole episode:

> I was downstairs when I heard Jeanne start screaming, "Get in here! Get in here now!" I ran up the stairs not knowing what to expect and saw two men sitting at the bar as plain as I am looking at you. They were white, but we could both see them plain as I can see you right now. They sat there for several seconds then they were gone.

When asked if Vance recognized who they may have been, pointing to a picture of the original owners, he confidently said, "I saw this guy and this guy."

The area of the bar where the owners saw the ghosts of two men. *Photo by Arlene Nicholson.*

Jeanne and Vance were very excited, as the security cameras were recording. "We were like; we are going to be millionaires. We just filmed two ghosts sitting at the bar." When they played the tape back, they saw no one but themselves and their reactions during the incident. This event took place after another incident left Vance wondering about whether his new business was haunted. He had owned the building for only one day when he decided to go in early and begin straightening the place out. He unlocked the door, and as he approached the back of the main taproom, a box that was sitting in the middle of a table flew off and landed on the floor several feet away.

Vance also had this to relate: "I would go into the basement where the kitchen and storage are, and I would hear footsteps and banging upstairs. I would say 'It's OK I am going to take care of you.' And the noises would cease."

A former bartender named Honey was often the object of the ghost's follies. Many times, she had her hair tugged while behind the bar. Thinking it was a patron, she would turn around and yell, "Knock it off!" only to realize there was no one there. "You could see her hair move and her head pull back as if someone was tugging on her hair," Vance stated.

Photograph of the original owners of the pub. The two men in the middle were the ones Jeanne and Vance witnessed sitting at the bar. *Photo by Arlene Nicholson.*

A few visits to Granville's Pub at the request of Jeanne and Vance proved most interesting. The second-floor function room seemed to be the place where the spirits lingered more than anywhere else in the building. This was the room where dances were held every Saturday night during the pub's heydays in the 1940s and '50s. Using dowsing rods to feel hot spots in areas about the room, Vance and Arlene proceeded to walk about. The rods began to wildly swing for both of them in the center of the room. An EMF detector was brought to that particular spot to take a reading, and the result was read aloud for the recorder to catalogue. Later, when the recording was reviewed, a voice could be heard saying, "Thaaats perfect."

During the vigil, a bell sounded. It was the exact sound a desk service bell makes when tapped. In old pubs, where the owner was the barkeep, cook, cleaner and whatnot, such bells were on the bar to summon him. Thirteen minutes later, the bell sounded again. A thorough investigation concluded that there was no such device in the room that could cause the echoing sound that we heard. When asked if there was someone that the spirits were looking for, a voice answered, "father."

Downstairs in the main taproom, Arlene asked, "I have one more question. Did you ring the bell upstairs?" At that moment the air around her became so cold that she related it to being in a freezer. This lasted for several seconds. Vance confessed that he experienced the same sudden icy cold spots in various areas of the building.

Granville's is not only a very friendly place but is well worth the small detour from the valley. If you do not witness a ghost, you can at least indulge in Vance's special Bloody Mary. Either way, Granville's Pub is definitely on the menu of haunted places to visit.

PAXTON

MOORE STATE PARK

Parks are full of wonderful sights and surprises. In Moore State Park, one of those sights may not be for the faint of heart. The 737-acre park was once home to water-powered mills in the eighteenth and nineteenth centuries. The first grist and sawmills sprang up along the brook in 1747. Turkey Hill Brook, which cascades ninety feet over a four-hundred-foot length, was perfect for providing the power that ran these mills.

Along with the mills stood a small village. Remnants of the settlement are still visible and include the trip hammer, schoolhouse, quarry and tavern. Other remnants make themselves known on occasion inside the renovated sawmill along the brook. These are the visages of three ghostly figures seen hanging from the beams of the mill. The ghosts are that of a young man and woman who committed suicide by hanging themselves from a beam of the structure. The other ghost is said to be a former owner of the mill. When he was hit with hard times, it was more than he could bear and thus took his own life in the mill.

FIRST CONGREGATIONAL CHURCH

The First Congregational Church in Paxton, Massachusetts, was erected in 1767, with Silas Bigelow as its first minister. Although he was well loved, his tenure in the church was short-lived. At only thirty years old, Silas was struck with the hand of death while delivering a sermon in the meetinghouse in 1769.

In 1830, the congregation broke ties with the town, becoming its own entity called the First Parish. In 1835, the building was moved to its present location with the financial assistance of the town, then repaired and renovated. It was around this time that the former minister began to haunt the newly restored house of worship.

The church is still haunted by the deceased minister. Candles mysteriously ignite in the chapel, and footsteps are often heard going up a set of stairs that no longer exists. Either he is unhappy about the move that took place so long ago, or he is still clinging to the ministry he helped establish during his short mortal span on this earth.

ANNA MARIA COLLEGE

The Sisters of St. Anne founded Anna Maria College in 1946 as a liberal arts college of higher education for women. The original location was in Marlborough, Massachusetts. In 1952, the college moved to its present location, becoming a coed school shortly after. The institution offers thirty-five undergraduate majors, twenty-one graduate programs and continuing education programs. The 190-acre campus is set in the beautiful rural town of Paxton, and like most other colleges in the region, it has its own school spirits.

One place of paranormal interest is Zecco Performing Arts Center in Founders Hall. The theater has a resident ghost the students affectionately named Theresa. Supposedly, during the building of the hall, the skeleton of a woman was unearthed and removed to the local cemetery. It is reported that her spirit is not at rest because the place she was moved from was her long-gone homestead.

Some claim that the skeleton was found under the stage during renovations. No one had any idea as to the identity of the remains. The legend sometimes includes that she was found with the skeletal remains of a baby in her arms. Whatever the case, Theresa likes to make herself known on occasion by placing an icy hand on the shoulders of patrons in the audience. Guests have also had an unseen entity brush by them, sometimes hitting their knees as if making its way toward one of the seats in the row they are seated in. Theresa likes to play with the theater lights as well. The lights will flicker, change color or turn off while no one is near the switches or controls.

Theresa is not the only ghost to reside at the college. A ghost named Betty haunts the Miriam Hall Music Building. Emma Nadeau, a student at the college, had several experiences with Betty. One night, she was alone in the hall with her friend. They occupied two of the practice rooms next to each other and were constantly interrupted by the slamming of the doors in the hall. Each time they investigated, they found no one but each other present in the building.

> *One night it was just my friend and me in the music rooms, yet we heard the door open and close several times. When we went to see who it was, the room was always empty. We continued to practice, and the door opened and closed again this time followed by footsteps. We were spooked at that point and left. People always have the same experience in the hall, especially at night when it is quiet.*

Lights constantly turn on and off, sometimes right in front of people in the rooms. Betty was obviously a musician, as she also has a habit of playing the piano. The piano will begin to play at random times with no visible hands touching the keys. She also likes to open and close the windows in the practice rooms. Voices are often heard, and upon examination, the place will be void of the living.

There are underground tunnels that were used by the students to get from one building to another during inclement weather. One section of the tunnels is haunted. You may have already guessed that it is the section that connects Miriam Hall with another, Madonna Hall. According to sources, that portion of the tunnel collapsed during construction, killing a few of the workers. Their spirits still remain in the tunnel where their mortal frames breathed their last breaths.

A DAY TO REMEMBER

In conclusion, we would like to relate one last tale. This event was not confined to the Blackstone Valley. All of New England and parts outward experienced what came to be known as the Dark Day of New England.

May 19, 1780, began dark and dreary. Many felt the unusually gloomy sky signaled a stormy day for the region, but they were about to experience an event that still baffles some scientists and historians to this day. A shadowy, sinister haze drifted overhead, eventually blocking out the sun, and within a few hours, the skies turned as black as midnight. In Connecticut, a farmer by the name of Joseph Joslin was working on his stone fence when the darkness set in. He was forced to suspend his task for want of light. Another farmer had to stop shoveling manure, as he could not "discern the difference between the ground and the dung." Even General Washington, encamped in nearby New Jersey, made note in his diary the night before that the skies had an unnatural look about them.

By the time clocks struck the hour of noon, the region, including eastern Canada, had fallen into a pitch black. Night birds began to sing, and other nocturnal animals, confused, emerged from their slumber. Cattle returned to their barns, and chickens refused to leave their roosts. Crickets began to sing, and frogs started their usual nightly sonatas. Turmoil and fear soon set in around the region, as the general populace became convinced that judgment day was upon them.

People were forced to move about by candlelight in the foreboding blackness. Connecticut councilman Abraham Davenport, grandson of the famous Reverend Jonathon Davenport of New Haven, staunchly defied recessing the council meeting despite the darkness.

The 19th of May, 1780, was a remarkable dark day. Candles were lighted in many houses, the birds were silent and disappeared....A very general opinion prevailed, that the Day of Judgment was at hand. The House of Representatives, being unable to transact their business adjourned....When the opinion of Mr. Davenport was asked, he answered "I am against an adjournment. The day of judgment is either approaching, or it is not. If it is not, there is no cause for an adjournment: if it is, I choose to be found doing my duty. I wish therefore that candles may be brought."

The diary of Mrs. Mary Holyoke stated, "Uncommon dark. Began at 10 A.M. Dind [dined] by candlelight." Dinner was what we now refer to as lunch. As the day progressed, the prevailing assumption that judgment day had finally come began to fade in the minds of the people. By nightfall, the light of the stars began to poke through the clearing murkiness, and a collective sigh of relief came over the land. New England's dark day had passed but would forever be remembered, even immortalized in poetry and prose through the eras.

BIBLIOGRAPHY

Acciardo, Linda. *Ghost of an Indian Maiden Haunts Tarkiln Woods.* Smithfield, RI: Observer Publications, 1983.

Andrews, Evan. "Remembering New England's 'Dark Day.'" History, May 19, 2015, https://www.history.com/news/remembering-new-englands-dark-day.

Arnold, James. *Vital Records of Rhode Island.* Providence, RI: Narragansett Historical Publishing Company, 1892.

Ballou, Adin. *An Elaborate History and Genealogy of the Ballous in America.* Providence, RI: Proprietary Publishers, 1888.

Bell, Michael E. *Food for the Dead.* New York: Carroll and Graf Publishers, 2001.

Botkin, B.A. *A Treasury of New England Folklore.* New York: Bonanza Books, 1995.

Bromley, Seth. *A Real Ghost Story.* Smithfield, RI: Observer Publications, 2003.

Cahill, Robert Ellis. *New England's Ancient Mysteries.* Salem, MA: Old Saltbox Publishing House Inc., 1993.

Clauson, James Earl. *These Plantations.* Providence, RI: E.A. Johnson Company, 1937.

D'Agostino, Thomas. *Abandoned Villages and Ghost Towns of New England.* Atglen, PA: Schiffer Publishing, 2008.

———. *Haunted Massachusetts.* Atglen, PA: Schiffer Publishing, 2006.

———. *Haunted Rhode Island.* Atglen, PA: Schiffer Publishing, 2006.

————. *Rhode Island's Haunted Ramtail Factory.* Charleston, SC: The History Press, 2014.

Gleeson, Alice Collins. *Colonial Rhode Island.* Pawtucket, RI: Automobile Journal Publishing, 1926.

Hayward, John. *The New England Gazatteer.* 8th ed. Concord, NH: Israel S. Boyd and William White, 1839.

Holyoke, Mary Vial. *The Holyoke Diaries 1708–1856.* Salem, MA: Essex Institute, 1911.

Ignasher, Jim. *Smithfield's Lost City. The Story of Hanton City and Its People.* Smithfield, RI: Self-published, 2005.

Longeway, Charles. *Worcester's Forgotten Catacombs.* Worcester, MA: C.W. Longeway Sr., 2015.

Lovecraft, H.P. *Selected Letters.* Sauk City, WI: Arkham House, 1964.

Matthews, Margery I. *Peleg's Last Word.* Foster, RI: Cardinal Press, 1987.

Mavor, James W., and Byron E. Dix. *Manitou: The Sacred Landscape of New England's Native Civilization.* Rochester, VT: Inner Traditions International, 1989.

Nutting, George. *Massachusetts. A Guide to Its Places and People.* Cambridge, MA: Riverside Press, 1937.

Ocker, J.W. *The New England Grimpendium.* Woodstock, VT: Countryman Press, 2010.

Perron, Andrea. *House of Darkness: House of Light.* Bloomington, IN: Author House Publishing, 2011.

Perry, Amos. *Rhode Island State Census, 1885.* Providence, RI: E.L. Freeman and Sons, 1887.

Revai, Cheri. *Haunted Massachusetts.* Mechanicsburg, PA: Stackpole Books, 2005.

Robinson, Charles Turek. *The New England Ghost Files.* North Attleborough, MA: Covered Bridge Press, 1994.

Smitten, Susan. *Ghost Stories of New England.* Auburn, WA: Ghost House Books, 2003

Tanner, M.O. "Exploring 'The Rumbly.'" *Observer* 17, no. 13 (May 1972).

————. "Hanton City Revisited." *Observer* 17, no. 24 (August 1972).

Walmsley, Amasa E. *Life and Confession of Amasa E. Walmsley.* Providence, RI, 1832.

Other Sources

Joseph Bucklin Society. bucklinsociety.net.

National Park Service. "The Tree Root that Ate Roger Williams." https://www.nps.gov/rowi/learn/news/the-tree-root-that-ate-roger-williams.htm.

Rhode Island Road Trips. www.quahog.org.

Riseup Paranormal. www.riseupparanormal.com.

Tavern on Main. www.tavernonmainri.com.

USC Digital Folklore Archives. folklore.usc.edu.

ABOUT THE AUTHORS

THOMAS D'AGOSTINO and ARLENE NICHOLSON have been extensively studying and investigating paranormal accounts for over thirty-six years. Authors of over a dozen books, together they have penned and captured on film the best haunts and history New England has to offer.

Tom is a graduate of Rhode Island College with a degree in political science. Tom builds his own musical instruments, many from the medieval and Renaissance eras.

Arlene is a professional photographer. Arlene's vast education spans from photography to marketing and fundraising. Arlene is also a talented tarot card reader with years of experience and success in the field.

Tom and Arlene work together with some of the best names in the field investigating the paranormal from New England and beyond.